"In a brief compass, Dr. Benge details the tremendous implications and eternal significance of the shedding of the blood of Jesus Christ. In so doing, he displays the heart of the gospel in all of its truth, beauty, simplicity, power, and awesomeness. Though a quick read, this book's rich content require deep meditation."

MICHAEL A.G. HAYKIN, chair and professor of church history, The Southern Baptist Theological Seminary in Louisville, Kentucky.

"In this book, Dustin Benge gives us a fresh glimpse of those biblical words that shine like light rays on the cross, making the darkness of ignorance flee and enabling us to see the breadth and length and height and depth of God's love for his elect people. Meditating on Christ's atoning work always leaves you with a fresh sense of profound gratitude for God's grace and reignites holy energy in worship. This book will do that for you!"

CONRAD MBEWE, pastor of Kabwata Baptist Church and founding chancellor of the African Christian University in Lusaka, Zambia.

"Not since John Murray's classic book *Redemption Accomplished and Applied* has there been a more readily accessible, doctrinally rich, and beautifully written work than what Dustin Benge has offered us in *The Precious Blood*. Discussions pertaining to the blood of Christ have been slowly sidelined over the years in contradiction to the timeless teaching of Scripture. Dustin wants to bring this discussion back into the light and shine it warmly on the hearts of those who need it most. I'm deeply grateful for this book and truly believe it will serve the Christian both doctrinally and devotionally."

> **NATE PICKOWICZ**, teaching pastor, Harvest Bible Church, Gilmanton Iron Works, New Hampshire.

"*The Precious Blood* is a deep yet accessible study on the blood of Christ. It will both stir your heart and lift your mind to heaven, where Christ is seated. After reading, you will be all the more thankful to Christ and even more resolved to live your life solely for him."

> **GRANT CASTLEBERRY**, senior pastor, Capital Community Church, Raleigh, North Carolina.

"The victory Jesus purchased for believers is a gift greater than we imagine. Much was accomplished by Christ on the cross, and it demands our deepest consideration and is worthy of our highest praise. In *The Precious Blood*, Dr. Benge humbly and pastorally walks the reader through the many facets of the gift God gave us when he offered his Son as payment for our sins. Christ's blood was sufficient; its results are profound. No Christian can read this book without closing its pages and immediately offering up a prayer of worship and gratitude."

MICHAEL STATON, pastor, First Baptist Mustang, Mustang, Oklahoma.

the
Precious
BLOOD

THE BENEFITS *of the*
ATONEMENT
of CHRIST

DUSTIN BENGE

H&E
Publishing

for

Cameron Dula

*"Friendship is one of the sweetest joys of life.
Many might have failed beneath the
bitterness of their trial had they
not found a friend."*

CHARLES H. SPURGEON

CONTENTS

Wonder-Working Power

MT. ZION BAPTIST CHURCH WAS AN enormous part of my childhood. A small, red-bricked building with a white steeple nestled in a valley of the Appalachian foothills of eastern Kentucky, it became a staple in my spiritual nurture. I can still recall my grandfather, Bert McCollum, standing beside the black upright piano while leading the congregation in the hymn "There's Power in the Blood."

Written by Lewis Edgar Jones in 1899, the chorus wafted through the rafters of that country church where generations of my family had gathered for worship each Lord's Day:

> There is power, power, wonder-working power
> In the blood of the Lamb.
> There is power, power, wonder-working power
> In the precious blood of the Lamb.

Several questions arise when meditating upon these seemingly simple words: What is this *wonder-working power* in the blood of the Lamb? Why is this blood *precious*? How can such *precious blood* be appropriated in my life?

The mention of *blood* as paramount in the Christian life is a sure sign that one is not attuned to modern sensitivities. After all, blood can be ghoulish and morbid, eliciting images of suffering and death. The sight of even a drop of blood causes many to become nauseous. Therefore, generally speaking, there is implied agreement that in polite conversation, people should avoid the topic altogether.

The fading mention of blood from church pulpits, in modern hymns and worship songs, or even within Christian vocabulary at large is a sure sign that we stand in desperate need of such power to be restored in our churches corporately and our hearts individually. When we remove the blood, we lose the wonder of the crucified Lamb and therefore forfeit the very core of what makes the gospel actually "good news."

The author of Hebrews reminds us that "without the shedding of blood there is no forgiveness" (Heb. 9:22). While it may seem ghastly to some, for all believers in Christ the blood is the life-giving ointment of new birth, transformation, and forgiveness. The blood of Christ reminds us that God, before the foundation of the world, chose to send his Son Jesus Christ to die a substitutionary death to rescue sinners from their sin. Seventeenth-century Puritan pastor Thomas Goodwin wrote, "Before the wound [of sin] was given, [God] provided a plaster and sufficient remedy to salve all again, which otherwise had been past finding out. For we, who could never have found out the remedy for a cut finger (had not God prescribed and appointed one), could much less for this life."[1] Even before sin entered the human story, God, in his sovereign providence, provided the remedy in the persn of his Son, Jesus Christ.

---

1   Thomas Goodwin, "Reconciliation by the Blood of Christ," in *The Works of Thomas Goodwin* (Grand Rapids: Reformation Heritage Books, 2006), 5:501.

In *A Puritan Theology*, Joel Beeke and Mark Jones outline the Puritan understanding of a "threefold cleansing" through the blood of Christ:

First, there was an objective cleansing of believers in Christ's death and resurrection. Puritan theologians argued for a subjective cleansing: the moment when the soul passes from death to life by embracing Christ's merits in faith. Finally, they asserted that a sensible cleansing wherein the Holy Spirit sprinkles Christ's blood on the soul to make the soul conscious that it is washed clean, is forgiven of all its trespasses, and has a right to eternal life.[2]

Though believers recognize the importance of Christ's death in the grand scheme of God's redemptive history, we rarely grasp its full potency in every aspect of our salvation and sanctification. The blood of Christ, representative of his death, isn't just applicable to the sinner in need of cleansing; it is also vitally necessary for our assurance and faithful perseverance. In other words, the power of Christ's blood through his death produces wonder after wonder in the Christian life and never stops flowing from the divine

2   Joel R. Beeke and Mark Jones, *A Puritan Theology: Doctrine for Life* (Grand Rapids, MI: Reformation Heritage Books, 2012), 361.

fountain of eternal love. Without Christ's blood, "we are of all people most to be pitied" (1 Cor. 15:19).

English Puritan Isaac Ambrose also points out the necessity of Christ's blood:

> It is the blood of Christ that rends the veil and makes a way into the holy of holies, that is, into the kingdom of heaven; without this blood there is no access to God; it is only by the blood of Christ that heaven is open to our prayers and that heaven is open to our persons. This blood is the key that unlocks heaven and lets in the souls of his redeemed ones.[3]

In *The Precious Blood*, I aim to examine various benefits of Christ's atonement—redemption, propitiation, cleansing, forgiveness, access, justification, sanctification, glorification, victory—and draw a single, blood-stained thread to unveil the glory of Christ, the Lamb. The Epilogue is the gospel—a complete presentation of the good news of salvation. This is to remind believers what the gospel is and to equip them to

---

3   Isaac Ambrose, *Looking unto Jesus* (repr., Harrisonburg, VA: Sprinkle Publications, 1986), 384.

share it with others while also presenting the good news to an unbeliever who may read this book.

The Precious Blood can be used for personal edification, small group Bible study, and as an evangelistic tool. I implore you, as Peter did his readers, to know "that you were ransomed from the futile ways inherited from your forefathers, not with perishable things such as silver or gold, but with *the precious blood of Christ*, like that of a lamb without blemish or spot" (1 Pet. 1:18–19).

1

Redemption

*In him we have redemption through his
blood, the forgiveness of our trespasses,
according to the riches of his grace.*

EPHESIANS 1:7

THERE ARE CERTAIN TRUTHS THAT NOT ONLY need
to be proclaimed but also enjoyed—doctrines that not only
transform our lives but alter our eternal destiny. One such
doctrine is salvation, the message of which transforms men
and women from a worldly rabble into the beautiful bride
of Christ.

The epicenter of salvation is the cross and empty tomb
of the Lord Jesus Christ, where his blood flowed freely to

pay the ransomed price for the rescue of sinners. The apostle Paul clearly declares the gospel of salvation in 1 Corinthians 15:3–4, "that Christ died for our sins in accordance with the Scriptures, that he was buried, that he was raised on the third day in accordance with the Scriptures."

The necessity of salvation could scarcely be put more categorically than in Jesus' words to Nicodemus in John 3: "Truly, truly, I say to you, unless one is born again he cannot see the kingdom of God. ... Do not marvel that I said to you, 'You must be born again'" (vv. 3, 7). Jesus underscores the significance of these words with the emphatic repetition "truly, truly." This is a way of signaling "Pay attention to what I'm about to say, because it is critically important." There are many things that are important, but not all of them are indispensable. Being born again is indispensable, for without it you will be shut out of the kingdom of God. Jesus' words of salvation apply universally to all people in every culture and time.

Nicodemus misunderstands Jesus' words and replies, "How can a man be born when he is old? Can he enter a second time into his mother's womb and be born?" (John 3:4). He suggests that going back to the beginning and being born a second time may achieve Jesus' intended outcome. However, Jesus confirms that even the unlikely event of entering your mother's womb a second time will only accomplish the same result and leave you with the same need.

Jesus answers, "Unless one is born of water and the Spirit, he cannot enter the kingdom of God. That which is born of flesh is flesh, and that which is born of the Spirit is spirit" (John 3:5–6). The phrase "born of water" here is not referring to baptism. Rather, Jesus is referring to a prophecy concerning the Messiah in Ezekiel 36:25–26: "I will sprinkle clean water on you, and you will be clean…. And I will give you a new heart, and a new spirit I will put within you." In other words, when the Messiah comes, he will bring eternal cleansing, forgiveness, and spiritual regeneration. Jesus is saying that since you need regeneration, you must be born again. He then points to the One who brings that cleansing: "That which is born of the Spirit is spirit" (John 3:6). It's the Holy Spirit who resurrects our dead hearts and regenerates them to new life.

It's not a new beginning you need; it's a new nature and new life which you are incapable of achieving alone. Only by the work and power of the Holy Spirit is the salvation of Christ brought about in our hearts.

Perhaps you ask, "Why?" *Why* do we need to be born again? *Why* do we need to be saved?

A Slave to Sin

The human story is a mess.

Every person can offer a testimony of tragedy because of what sin has led us to do or has done to us. Sin is pervasive. It's in us and all around us. In short, sin defines our very existence.

Puritan pastor Richard Alleine explains sin as follows:

Sin is that insurrection and rebellion of the heart against God. It turns from him and turns against him; it runs over to the camp of the enemy and there takes up arms against God. Sin is a running from God and a fighting against God; it would spoil the Lord of all the jewels of his crown. It opposes the sovereignty of God. A sinful heart would set up itself on God's throne; it would be king in his stead and have the command of all.

Sinners would be their own gods.[1]

Even a cursory read of history teaches us that sin plagues humans from birth to death. Sin is a predominant theme that runs throughout the Bible. Every human being born since the disobedience and fall of Adam and Eve in Genesis 3 is enslaved to sin, under total captivity to a nature that is wholly corrupt, evil, and separated from God. To describe our human condition in the most vivid analogy possible, the Bible says we are "slaves" to sin.

Slavery has a long and disgusting history and was commonly practiced across the known ancient world. Within the Roman Empire, enslaved people included prisoners of war, sailors captured and sold by pirates, and slaves bought outside the Roman territory. In desperate times, it wasn't uncommon for Roman citizens in poverty to sell themselves into slavery or even sell or rent their children into slavery. All enslaved people and their families were the property of their owners, who could sell or rent them out to others and even kill them for any reason without punishment. In

---

1   Richard Alleine, *Heaven Opened* (London: The Religious Tract Society, 1831), 190.

bondage to this cruel and inhuman existence, slaves were often whipped, branded, and cruelly mistreated. It's no mistake that Scripture uses the brutal life of an enslaved person as a picture of our sinful nature. Jesus said, "Truly, truly, I say to you, everyone who practices sin is a *slave* to sin" (John 8:34).

This same dreadful imagery is employed by Paul, who describes us as "slaves of sin" (Rom. 6:20). As such, we have no possibility of freeing ourselves from these enslaving shackles by which we are bound.

The Bible teaches that we are not sinners because we sin; we sin because we are sinners. In other words, we are all born spiritually dead with a sinful, depraved nature. The Old Testament prophet Isaiah wrote, "All we like sheep have gone astray; we have turned—every one—to his own way" (Isa. 53:6). The prophet Jeremiah laments, "The heart is deceitful above all things, and desperately sick; who can understand it?" (Jer. 17:9). Bottom line: "None is righteous, no, not one; no one understands; no one seeks for God" (Rom. 3:10–11). No human being has the power to escape or set himself free from his inherent nature. This is why Jesus told Nicodemus in John 3 that we must be "born again." We all stand condemned before God in our sin, for it is our owner, and we are its slave. A price must be paid for our freedom.

The Hope of the World

Attending a slave auction in the Roman Forum would have been similar to perusing a used car lot today. The Forum was a marketplace where slaves were put on public display for inspection before an auction occurred. An enslaved person's potential price was assessed before the auction started. Roman law dictated that masters divulge the ethnic origin of the slaves they were offering for sale and be forthright about any defects they might possess. Slaves were held in iron cages or wooden pens to prevent escape, and the sound of the whip could be heard cracking in the air, threatening punishment if they didn't cooperate with the scrutiny of those interested in making a purchase.

The bodies of the slaves were fully inspected, and their teeth examined. Plaques or placards hung around their necks detailing their good and bad qualities, abilities for work, origin, and nationality. Once the auction began, the traders emphasized their features and why they should fetch a specific price. Often displayed on platforms or revolving stands, some were stripped naked so the buyers knew exactly what they were purchasing. Once the auction commenced, the slave was sold to the highest bidder. Transitioning from the possession of one to the control of another, a slave lived a cyclical, hopeless existence.

Redemption was the only hope for a slave.

The Bible teaches that we all stand exposed in the slave market of sin, utterly incapable of saving or freeing ourselves from our inherent nature. Yet within the biblical word "redemption" is our hope.

Throughout Scripture, the central theme of redemption is the good news that God has taken the initiative to act graciously on behalf of those who are powerless to help themselves—you and me. Redemption involves God's recognition and identification with persons in their natural condition and his securing their emancipation from the captivity of sin through the obedience, suffering, death, and resurrection of his beloved Son, Jesus Christ.

Redemption means paying a ransom for something that has been lost, thereby purchasing it back. The Greek word *apolutrōsis* is found ten times in the New Testament, with nine of those translated as "redemption" and one translated as "release." Each time this word occurs, it has the idea of paying a required ransom price for an enslaved person found at auction.

In the Old Testament, God wrote into his law that when an Israelite sold himself into slavery because of poverty, his family must have an opportunity to ransom him back by paying the price—the price of redemption. The law states, "After he is sold he may be *redeemed*. One of his brothers may *redeem* him, or his uncle or his cousin may *redeem* him, or a close relative from his clan may *redeem* him" (Lev. 25:48–49). The word "redeem" is the Hebrew word *ga'al*, which means to act as a redeemer to ransom by payment. David, the psalmist, used the same word as a name for God: "Let the words of my mouth and the meditation of my heart be acceptable in your sight, O LORD, my rock and my *redeemer*" (Ps. 19:14). David's meditation has taken him back to God's redemption of his people Israel from Egyptian bondage.

God is a redeemer.

How does God redeem? What does God use to purchase his people out of the slave market of sin? Paul tells us in Ephesians, "In [Christ] we have *redemption* through his *blood*" (Eph. 1:7). Blood is equivalent to death, and death is the penalty and price of our sin (Rom. 6:23). God redeems us from the bondage of our sin through the death of Christ. Paul reminds us in 1 Corinthians 6:20, "For you were bought with a price." What price? Peter answers in 1 Peter 1:18–19: "You were ransomed from the futile ways inherited from your forefathers, not with perishable things such as silver or gold, but with the *precious blood of Christ*, like that of a lamb without blemish or spot."

This is the purpose for which Christ came to earth, "to give his life as a ransom for many" (Matt. 10:28; Mark 10:45). Christ freely gave his blood and became our substitute in death to redeem us from what we deserved. He made an infinite payment by offering his own "precious blood," through which we have redemption from the captivity of our sin.

In the Old Testament, for thousands of years, the blood of animals was offered as a temporary atonement for sin upon the altars of the wilderness tabernacle and Jerusalem temple. That ocean of blood was never sufficient to eternally cleanse anyone of sin. The author of Hebrews writes, "For it is impossible for the blood of bulls and goats to take away sins" (Heb. 10:4), but when God's spotless Lamb offered his life as payment, "we have been sanctified ... once for all" (Heb. 10:10).

The death of Christ was so satisfactory to God in appeasing his holy wrath against sin and paying the price required for redemption that his blood was a "fragrant aroma" (Eph. 5:2, NASB). As a reward for paying the required price of all those who will ever believe, "when Christ had offered for all time a single sacrifice for sins, he sat down at the right hand of God" (Heb. 10:12).

Seventeenth-century English pastor George Swinnock says, "God is incomparable in the work of redemption." He goes on to define redemption as

his masterpiece, pure workmanship; and indeed, all his works of creation and providence are subordinate to this. All his attributes sparkle most gloriously in this (Ps. 102:16); all his angels in heaven admire and adore him for this (Rev. 4:10–11). This is the work of all his works, which he is so mightily pleased with and reaps so much glory and praise from (Isa. 42:1; 43:21). ...

None besides God had pity enough for man's misery, or wisdom enough to find out a remedy, or power enough for his recovery. None had pity enough for man's misery. Boundless misery called for boundless mercy. ... But where is such mercy to be found among the creatures? Man was a child of wrath, had plunged himself into an ocean of evils and fury, and this required an ocean of love and pity. ... But the creator had infinite grace for infinite guilt and infinite mercy for infinite misery.[2]

Here is what we have learned so far:

1. The price of our sin is death.
2. The price of our redemption was the lifeblood of the perfect, spotless Lamb of God, Jesus Christ, God's only Son.
3. No other price but Christ's perfect blood in his death could have paid our eternal sin debt.
4. Christ receives all glory and honor at God's right hand because he paid the perfect price by his death.
5. Those whom Christ has purchased from the slave

---

2   George Swinnock, *The Incomparableness of God*, in *The Works of George Swinnock* (Edinburgh: The Banner of Truth Trust, 1992), 4:432.

market of sin have been resurrected from their dead condition to become slaves of righteousness.

As slaves, shackled to our sin, we are displayed on the block in the marketplace.

No hope of freedom.

No hope of life.

No hope of redemption.

But out of nowhere, at the precise time, a Man steps forward and says, "I will pay their ransom price with my own blood and freely offer my life as a substitute in death that they may be redeemed." This Man, our Lord Jesus Christ, is then bound and crucified on a cross as payment for our sin.

It is through the precious blood of Christ that God rescues us and delivers "us from the domain of darkness and transfer[s] us to the kingdom of his beloved Son" (Col. 1:13). It is no wonder that a number that no one can count will eternally praise the Lamb before his glorious throne for his redeeming work:

Worthy are you to take the scroll and to open its seals, for you were slain, and by your blood you ransomed people for God from every tribe and language and people and nation, and you have made them a kingdom and priests to our God, and they shall reign on the earth. (Rev. 5:9–10)

SCRIPTURE

Ezekiel 36:25–27; John 3:1–20; Romans 5;
Ephesians 2:1–10

REFLECTION

1. Why do human beings require redemption?
2. What does it mean that we are slaves to sin?
3. What is the required price for redemption, and how is that appropriated in our lives?
4. How does God act as a redeemer?
5. Why does God accept the death of Jesus Christ as a sacrifice for our sin?

2

Propitiation

All who believe ... are justified ... through the redemption
that is in Christ Jesus, whom God put forward as a
propitiation by his blood, to be received by faith. This
was to show God's righteousness, because in his divine
forbearance he had passed over former sins.

ROMANS 3:22, 24–25

THE SACRIFICE OF CHRIST UPON THE CROSS is one
of those theological diamonds for which—no matter how
many times we examine it—new facets of beauty are always
being revealed. As many have said, the waters of the gospel
are like a vast ocean in which we can plunge to the depths
but we cannot reach the bottom.

The Bible speaks of Christ's death not simply as a sacrifice but as a *propitiatory* sacrifice. The word "propitiation" is a theological term which means averting the wrath of God by the offering of a gift. On the cross, Jesus Christ received the full outpouring of his Father's righteous wrath against the sins of his people, and with his own blood, he satisfied God's just anger against sin and diverted God's wrath from us to himself. A simple way to understand this is to say Christ became our substitute.

We need a propitiator.

God's Righteous Wrath

The idea of God's wrath is a foreign topic nowadays. In fact, even to mention God's wrath is to evoke rejection by our hearers. "God would never be that harsh." "I thought God was love, not wrath." "Surely God wouldn't send anyone to hell." "Doesn't God say that he loves sinners?" These are but a few of the prevalent objections to this divine attribute that so often offends modern sensibilities.

Our problem with God's wrath springs from the fact that we consider wrath in human categories rather than divine. That is, we conclude that God must be like us when he expresses his wrath, a morally monstrous and vindictive person who threatens, "You just watch out—I'm going to get you!" But this is not the God of Scripture, for God's wrath is in perfect accord with his perfect righteousness, holiness, and justice. God can't be divided into various parts, as if he had multiple personalities. Since he is both infinite mercy and infinite justice, this requires that every single one of our sins committed against his infinite holiness be punished. Paul reminds us: "The wages of sin is death, but the free gift of God is eternal life in Christ Jesus our Lord" (Rom. 6:23).

The biblical authors do not shy away from speaking of God's wrath. Both the Old and New Testaments reveal countless verses that describe the wrath of God:

God is a righteous judge, and a God who feels indignation every day. (Ps. 7:11)

I will execute great vengeance on them with wrathful rebukes. Then they will know that I am the Lord, when I lay my vengeance upon them. (Ezek. 25:17)

The Lord is a jealous and avenging God; the Lord is

avenging and wrathful; the LORD takes vengeance on his adversaries and keeps wrath for his enemies. (Nah. 1:2)

Whoever believes in the Son has eternal life; whoever does not obey the Son shall not see life, but the wrath of God remains on him. (John 3:36)

For the wrath of God is revealed from heaven against all ungodliness and unrighteousness of men, who by their unrighteousness suppress the truth. (Rom. 1:18)

While some divide God into a wrathful Old Testament "tyrant" and a benevolent New Testament "daddy," a consistent reading of both Testaments discerns that the presentation of God's wrath is wholly consistent throughout Scripture. J. I. Packer rightly states: "God's wrath in the Bible is never the capricious, self-indulgent, irritable, morally ignoble thing that human anger so often is. It is, instead, a right and necessary reaction to objective moral evil."[1]

There is no greater portrait of divine love than when God

---

1   J. I. Packer, *Knowing God* (Downers Grove, IL: IVP Books, 1973), 151.

poured his wrath out upon his beloved Son at Calvary. On the cross, God unleashed his holy fury upon our sin-bearer and substitute, Jesus Christ, who became for us "a propitiation by his blood" (Rom. 3:25). The good news is that "Christ Jesus came into the world to save sinners" (1 Tim. 1:15).

Jesus is our Propitiator.

Propitiation

The word *propitiation* may be foreign to you, as many Bible readers give it nothing more than a passing thought. The New Testament only uses the word a handful of times. The noun form appears in two verses:

> He is the *propitiation* for our sins.... (1 John 2:2)

> In this is love, not that we have loved God but that he loved us and sent his Son to be the *propitiation* for our sins. (1 John 4:10)

The verb form, "to propitiate," is also found in two verses. In the story of the Pharisee and the tax collector in Luke

18, the word is translated "merciful" in verse 13; the tax collector beats his breast in prayer before God and requests, "God, be *merciful* to me, a sinner!" The word is used again in Hebrews 2:17: "Therefore [Jesus Christ] had to be made like his brothers in every respect, so that he might become a *merciful* and faithful high priest in the service of God, to make propitiation for the sins of the people."

In addition, there are two occurrences indicating *propitiation* used in different forms in the New Testament. In Hebrews 9:5, the word is translated "mercy seat." The mercy seat was the gold covering over the ark of the covenant that sat in the holy of holies in the Old Testament tabernacle during Israel's wilderness wanderings. The written law of God had been placed in the ark of the covenant as a perpetual reminder of the reality of our sin against God's righteous standard. The mercy seat was the place the high priest would sprinkle the blood of sacrifice to atone for the sins of the people. The mercy seat became the place of atonement that covered sin, representing God covering our sinful guilt through his promised Redeemer.

Again, in Paul's letter to the church in Rome, we discover the word *propitiation* used in reference to the blood of

Christ. Paul writes, "... through the redemption that is in Christ Jesus, whom God put forward as a propitiation by his blood, to be received by faith. This was to show God's righteousness, because in his divine forbearance he had passed over former sins" (Rom. 3:24–25). When the Old Testament priests offered the blood of sacrifices, they were symbolically covering over sin (Lev. 4:35; 10:17; 16:30). In this sense, propitiation is a covering of sin to hide that which is offensive in order to remove God's wrath as the offended party. Like the author of Hebrews, Paul identifies Jesus as our High Priest who, with his own blood, removes our sinful offense by taking upon himself the holy wrath of God against our sin.

Jesus is our propitiation and eternally performs what the priests of the Old Testament were foreshadowing. Every sacrifice in the Old Testament points to the ultimate sacrifice of Christ on the cross, where he freely gave his own blood to pay the debt sinners owe to God for offending his holiness. Christ's work of propitiation eternally covers the guilt of sinners by satisfying God's justice and turning away God's wrath against sin.

In summary, seventeenth-century Puritan theologian

John Owen lists four essential elements in propitiation:

1. An offense to be taken away. (Our sin)
2. A person offended who needs to be pacified. (God)
3. An offending person; one guilty of the offense. (Sinners)
4. A sacrifice or some other means of making atonement for the offense. (Jesus Christ)[2]

The doctrine of propitiation simply means that God so loved the objects of his wrath that he gave his only begotten Son that through his perfect blood he would make provision for the removal of his wrath. Christ so wholly satisfies God's wrath that those who were once objects of his wrath are now beloved children.

Reconciliation

In the New Testament, the word *propitiation* means the same thing as *atonement* and *reconciliation*. Often, they are used interchangeably. Within the word *reconciliation*, we

2   John Owen, *An Exposition of the Epistle to the Hebrews* (Edinburgh: The Banner of Truth Trust, 2009), 3:476.

discover the trajectory of God's redemptive plan.

After Adam and Eve sinned in the garden, they immediately hid from God and were subsequently driven from his presence, creating an impassible chasm between sinful man and a holy God (Gen. 3:22–24). Not only did man fall from a state of innocence, but the universe fell from perfection, plunging into a cursed state. If God did not intervene, man would die and enter hell, and the universe would eventually become a wasteland, as the consequence of this sinful curse is ultimately death.

The prophet Isaiah speaks of this tragic separation: "But your iniquities have made a separation between you and your God, and your sins have hidden his face from you so that he does not hear" (Isa. 59:2). This separation is infinitely large and cannot be bridged through the achievement of any good works or self-righteous holiness. Even when humans fell, in the pronouncement of the curse upon them, God speaks of his plan of reconciliation (Gen. 3:15).

The verb "to reconcile" means "to change" or "exchange." Three times this word is used in the New Testament to indicate a change in relationship. In 1 Corinthians 7:11, Paul employs this word to speak of a woman being reconciled with her husband. And the two other usages speak of God being reconciled to man (Rom. 5:10; 2 Cor. 5:18–20). The heart of the word *reconciliation* is the restoration of a right relationship between God and man.

In Colossians 1:20, Paul uses a more intense word for reconcile that means "thoroughly, completely, or totally reconciled." Combating false teachers who denied that Christ alone was sufficient for reconciliation with God, Paul reminds the church that not only is Christ enough, but he brings total, complete, and full reconciliation between God and man. Listen to Paul's words:

> For in him all the fullness of God was pleased to dwell, and through him to reconcile to himself all things, whether on earth or in heaven, making peace by the blood of his cross. And you, who once were alienated and hostile in mind, doing evil deeds, he has now reconciled in his body of flesh by his death, in order to present you holy and blameless and above reproach before him. (Col. 1:19–22)

God made peace with us (reconciliation) through the

blood of Christ (propitiation)—all for the purpose of presenting us "holy and blameless" to himself. Through the cross, God is gathering his people from every corner of the earth. We who were his enemies are now his friends.

The Heart of the Gospel

In his timeless work *Knowing God*, J. I. Packer defines propitiation as the heart of the gospel. He states:

> The word "propitiation" is the central heart of the Gospel; in the faith of the New Testament it is central. The love of God, the taking of human form by the Son, the meaning of the cross, Christ's heavenly intercession, the way of salvation... . In saying this, we swim against the stream of much modern teaching and condemn at a stroke the views of a great number of distinguished church leaders today, but we cannot help that. Paul wrote, "even if we or an angel from heaven"—let alone a minister, bishop, college lecturer, university professor, or noted author—"should preach a Gospel other than the one we preached to you, let him be eternally condemned!" (Gal. 1:8). A gospel without propitiation

at its heart is another gospel than that which Paul preached.[3]

God must punish sin. And for us, this would mean an eternity spent in hell. But what God requires, he provides in the person and work of his only begotten Son who becomes for us a wrath-bearing sacrifice. God doesn't overlook sin, turn a blind eye, or excuse it, for sin must be punished. Every ounce of wrath deserved by believers because of their sin is fully and eternally poured out on our substitute in those three terrible hours on Calvary.[4] Christ drank the cup of God's wrath, offering his blood on the cross, as our propitiation declaring our sins "paid in full!"

This is the gospel.

---

3   J. I. Packer, *Knowing God*, 180–199.
4   John MacArthur and Richard Mayhue, eds., *Biblical Doctrine* (Wheaton, IL: Crossway Books, 2017), 531.

SCRIPTURE

Isaiah 59:1–3; Nahum 1:2–15; Romans 3:21–26;
Colossians 1:15–23; 1 John 4:7–12

REFLECTION

1. How do we biblically define God's wrath?
2. Why must a penalty be paid for sin?
3. Given that man is separated from God because of sin, how does Christ bring us back to God?
4. Why is the blood of Christ sufficient to reconcile us to God?

3

Cleansing

The blood of Jesus his Son
cleanses us from all sin.

1 JOHN 1:7

IF NOTHING ELSE IS CLEAR AT THIS POINT, I would
have you to remember that our sinful nature has left
us dead and alienated from God. While we are in this
depraved state, we love to sin. The human story is one of
slavery and bondage to sin. However, the glorious promise
of the gospel is that we do not have to remain in that sin.
Though we struggle with sin until our last, dying breath,
we no longer have to feel the sting of its condemnation and
guilt. The gospel promises cleansing through the blood of

Christ—continually and eternally.

When Jesus girded himself with a towel, took a basin of water, and began to wash his disciples' feet, Simon Peter immediately objected:

> He came to Simon Peter, who said to him, "Lord, do you wash my feet?" Jesus answered him, "What I am doing you do not understand now, but afterward you will understand." Peter said to him, "You shall never wash my feet." Jesus answered him, "If I do not wash you, you have no share with me." Simon Peter said to him, "Lord, not my feet only but also my hands and my head!" Jesus said to him, "The one who has bathed does not need to wash, except for his feet, but is completely clean." (John 13:6–10)

Jesus was washing Peter's feet not merely because his feet were dirty from the dust of the Jerusalem roads, but as an illustration of cleansing. In just a matter of hours, Jesus would be arrested, tried, and crucified. On the cross, this illustration is brought to life through the shedding of Jesus' blood. John later writes, "The blood of Jesus his Son cleanses us from all sin" (1 John 1:7). Once Peter relented and agreed to have his feet washed, he implored Jesus to wash his whole body. Jesus did not protest the need for the washing of the whole body but said that if your body has already been washed, then your feet only need to be washed periodically (vv. 10–11).

Jesus emphasizes here a two-fold cleansing. When we are saved and our hearts regenerated, we are definitively and permanently cleansed from sin. This is the purpose for which Jesus shed his blood, to cleanse us of *all* sin. However, what are believers to do when they sin? Our sin as believers does not cast us out of the kingdom or require another "whole body" washing, but our sin still has to be dealt with. As a result, John calls for the necessity of cleansing:

> If we say we have no sin, we deceive ourselves, and the truth is not in us. If we confess our sins, he is faithful and just to forgive us our sins and to cleanse us from all unrighteousness. If we say we have not sinned, we make him a liar, and his word is not in us. (1 John 1:8–10)

The blood of Christ cleanses us of sin when we are

converted and keeps on cleansing us from sin after we're converted. We are both cleansed eternally at salvation and continually during sanctification. The blood of Christ is a never-ending fountain of divine love eternally washing our sin away.

Washing

The concept of "washing" is a repeated theme throughout Scripture. The children of Israel in the Old Testament were given numerous instructions and laws regarding ritual washing. The people were consecrated through washing their garments (Exod. 19:10–11). Aaron and his sons were set apart as priests through washing (Exod. 40:12–15). The Levites who served as priests in the tabernacle were purified through washing (Num. 8:5–7). Throughout the books of Leviticus and Numbers, the theme of *clean* and *unclean* was common.

The same theme extends to the New Testament. But rather than cleansing being a temporary act of purification like in the Old Testament, the dawning of the new covenant signals a transition from temporal to eternal. The incarnation of Christ inaugurates the coming of the kingdom of

God, so rather than temporary cleansing from sin until the next sacrifice, through the blood of Christ we are eternally cleansed from all the sin we have ever committed. Listen to the words of Paul:

> But when the goodness and loving kindness of God our Savior appeared, he saved us, not because of works done by us in righteousness, but according to his own mercy, by the washing of regeneration and renewal of the Holy Spirit, whom he poured out on us richly through Jesus Christ our Savior, so that being justified by his grace we might become heirs according to the hope of eternal life. (Titus 3:4–7)

Paul is quick to point out that no part of our salvation is a result of works, merit, or righteousness which we have done. Quite the contrary. "He saved us ... according to his own mercy, by the *washing* of regeneration and renewal of the Holy Spirit" (v. 5). Recall what Jesus told Nicodemus in John 3:5: "Unless one is born of *water* and the *Spirit*, he cannot enter the kingdom of God." Paul, writing to Titus, draws the same connection here—"by the *washing* of regeneration and renewal of the *Holy Spirit*." The promise of this washing appears in Ezekiel 36:25–27:

> I will sprinkle clean *water* on you, and you shall be clean from all your uncleannesses, and from all your idols I will cleanse you. And I will give you a new heart, and a new spirit I will put within you.... And I will put *my Spirit* within you, and cause you to walk in my statutes.

As already referenced in the first chapter, Ezekiel's prophecy comes to pass with the incarnation of Christ, who eternally cleanses us of all sin—past, present, and future—through the Holy Spirit. This doesn't mean we no longer struggle with our fight against sin, but it means that through the blood of Christ we are assured that "there is therefore now no condemnation for those who are in Christ Jesus" (Rom. 8:1).

In his "Discourse on the Cleansing Virtue of Christ's Blood," Puritan pastor Stephen Charnock describes the extent of our cleansing:

> [Christ's blood] cleanseth from all sin universally. For

since it was the blood of so great a person as the Son of God, it is as powerful to cleanse us from the greatest as the least. Had it been the blood of a sinful creature, it had been so far from expiation, that it would rather have been for pollution. Had it been the blood of an angel, though holy (supposing they had any to shed), yet it had been the blood of a creature, and therefore incapable of mounting to an infinite value; but since it is the blood of the Son of God, it is both the blood of a holy and of an uncreated and infinite person. Is it not therefore able to exceed all the bulk of finite sins, and to equal in dignity the infiniteness of the injury in every transgressor?[1]

Charnock presents four truths regarding the sufficiency of Christ's blood to cleanse:

It has a virtue to cleanse. "It does not actually cleanse all, but only those that believe," Charnock writes. In other words, medicine that is not taken should not be expected to

---

1   Stephen Charnock, "A Discourse on the Cleansing Virtue of Christ's Blood," in *The Works of Stephen Charnock* (Edinburgh: The Banner of Truth Trust, 2010), 3:518.

heal the sickness for which it was prescribed.

The blood of Christ cleanses, not has cleansed, or shall cleanse. The blood of Christ never stops cleansing us from sin. Charnock says, "It was shed but once, it is applied often, and the virtue of it is as durable as the person whose blood it is."

The blood of Christ cleanses. It's not Christ's blood plus something else. The blood of Christ "has the sole and the sovereign virtue." Therefore, there is no need to add merit, additional sacrifices, or even the false doctrine of purgatory. Anything added to the sufficiency of Christ's blood nullifies it altogether. The act of cleansing is reserved exclusively for Christ's blood; nothing is to be added.

The blood of Christ cleanses us from all sin. Charnock writes, "It absolves from the guilt of sin, and shelters from the wrath of God. ... This blood purges not some sort of sins and leaves the rest to be expiated by a purgatory fire." The perfection of Christ's blood is seen in the extent in which it cleanses—*all sin*.[2]

Jesus has washed us to the extent that we are released from

---

2   Stephen Charnock, "The Cleansing Virtue of Christ's Blood," in *Works*, 3:518.

our slavery to sin and are now set free to "live according to the Spirit" (Rom. 8:5).

Walk by the Spirit

Being cleansed from our sin doesn't give us the freedom to live any way we desire as believers. We're never given a license or liberty to sin. In Romans 6, Paul clarifies that believers are now slaves to another master, Christ: "Thanks be to God, that you who were once slaves of sin have become obedient from the heart to the standard of teaching to which you were committed, and, having been set free from sin, have become slaves of righteousness" (vv. 17–18). Now that we are "slaves of righteousness," we are commanded to "walk not according to the flesh but according to the Spirit" (Rom. 8:4). Now that we have been cleansed of sin, what does it mean to walk "according to the Spirit"?

Paul further explores this injunction of living by the Spirit in Galatians 5:

Walk by the Spirit (v. 16)
Be led by the Spirit (v. 18)
Bear the fruit of the Spirit (v. 22)

Live by the Spirit (v. 25)
Keep in step with the Spirit (v. 25)

Our cleansing through Christ's blood enables us to live by the Spirit. That refers to our daily walk, conduct, words, thoughts, and actions being rooted in the very life, death, resurrection, and ascension of Christ. Where sin once animated our lives in our rebellion against God because we have been cleansed, the Spirit is now animating our lives to produce godly fruit. The Spirit shapes our decisions, desires, and life direction.

A life characterized by Spirit-led living is continuously concerned with growing in Christlikeness, having our minds saturated with the truth of God's Word, having our hearts enraptured in perpetual doxology, giving our lives in service to love and help our neighbors, and glorifying the Lord in all things.

This is the purpose of our cleansing—living according to the Spirit.

SCRIPTURE

John 13:6–10; Romans 8:1–17; Galatians 5; Titus 3:4–7

REFLECTION

1. Why do believers require dual cleansing, both eternally in salvation and continually in sanctification?
2. What does it mean for a believer to "walk by the Spirit"?
3. List some practical ways in which you can walk by the Spirit and not by the flesh. What are some areas where you find this easy or difficult?
4. What role does confession of sins play in God's forgiveness of our sins and our ongoing sanctification?

4

Forgiveness

*Without the shedding of blood there is
no forgiveness of sins.*

ROMANS 9:22

IF WE CLAIM TO BE "SAVED," IT'S necessary to know from what.

The nature and significance of salvation is not fully realized until we recognize what we have been saved *from*. The apostle Paul helps us with this in Romans 5:9: "Since, therefore, we have now been justified by his blood, much more shall we be saved by him from the wrath of God."

Wrath? What a foreign concept in our modern context that waxes so eloquent on the love of God while completely dismissing his wrath as an arcane ancient concept! We seem to have forgotten that "the wages of sin is death" (Rom. 6:23) and "unless you repent, you will all likewise perish" (Luke 13:3). Our sin is heinous and treasonous before a holy God. Sin, according to the prophet Jeremiah, shocks and appalls the heavens:

> Be appalled, O heavens, at this;
>   be shocked, be utterly desolate,
> declares the LORD,
> for my people have committed two evils:
> they have forsaken me,
>   the fountain of living waters,
> and hewed out cisterns for themselves,
>   broken cisterns that can hold no water.
> (Jer. 2:12–13)

Sin is the forsaking of God and his righteous commandments: acting as if he doesn't exist, and if he exists, his laws do not apply to us. Yet whether we believe it or not, the wrath of God is coming against all sin and sinners (Col. 3:5–6). But those who have been saved, redeemed, and born again have a substitute who stood in our place to pay the full penalty of our sin—Jesus Christ.

Against the atrocity of our sin are the sweet words, "She will bear a son, and you shall call his name Jesus, for he will save his people from their sins" (Matt. 1:21). Into a morose world steps the Son of God who would willingly drink the full cup of God's unmitigated and holy wrath against sin. John rightly recognized him as "the Lamb of God, who takes away the sin of the world!" (John 1:29).

We are saved from God's wrath only through the blood of Christ. Hebrews 9:22 states, "Without the shedding of blood there is no forgiveness of sins."

What is our problem? We are sinners.

What is our need? We need to be forgiven of our sin.

Who can forgive sin? Only Jesus Christ.

How does Jesus forgive sin? Through the shedding of his blood.

Forgiveness Demands Blood

The concept of shed blood goes all the way back to the Old Testament. Blood is a symbol of death. In the old covenant, God instituted animal sacrifice as the symbol through which men and women could have their sins covered. In Exodus 24, Moses sprinkled blood on the altar and the people to inaugurate the covenant. The countless animal sacrifices that characterized this old system were a continual reminder that nothing short of death was the penalty for sin.

In the upper room, surrounded by his disciples the night before his death, Jesus takes a cup filled with wine and says, "This is my blood of the covenant, which is poured out for many for the forgiveness of sins" (Matt. 26:28). This cup signifies the place and means of our forgiveness. Reflecting on the frequency of the old covenant sacrificial system, the writer of Hebrews states, "Every priest stands daily at his service, offering repeatedly the same sacrifices, which can never take away sins" (Heb. 10:11). The old system was insufficient for full atonement and forgiveness. However, Jesus says, "This cup is the *new covenant* in *my* blood. Do this, as often as you drink it, in remembrance of me" (1 Cor. 11:25). The new covenant is God's eternal promise that "I will be merciful toward their iniquities, and I will remember their sins no more" (Heb. 8:12). Just as Moses inaugurated the old covenant through the blood of animals, the new covenant was inaugurated by Christ through his own blood.

It is incumbent upon us to acknowledge that a preoccupation with the physical aspects of Christ's death can lead to theological mistakes. In other words, there's no magical or mystical power in the physical blood of the incarnate Christ. It's not his physical blood in the material sense that is the foundation of our forgiveness. Instead, it's his dying in our place, as our substitute, which is symbolized by the pouring forth of his blood, that is the ground of our forgiveness. If it were merely his physical blood that saved us, he could have pricked his finger and avoided the cross altogether. But as Jesus confessed in the garden, there was no other way; death was imminent and necessary in God's redemptive plan. Jesus had to die.

Forgiveness is a dismissal and release of something. The forgiveness available to sinners in Christ involves the release of our sin from God's just wrath and penalty and the complete dismissal of all charges against us to the extent that "there is therefore now no condemnation for those who are in Christ Jesus" (Rom. 8:1).

Forgiveness is a deliberate act of grace, love, and mercy to not hold something against another person, despite what he or she has done. We have offended God's righteousness and holiness, but God holds no charge against us in Christ. Charles H. Spurgeon observes, "It is not redemption through his power; it is through his blood. It is not redemption through his love; it is through his blood. This is insisted upon emphatically, since in order to [have] forgiveness of sins it is redemption through his blood."[1]

How flippantly we regard forgiveness! We lie, ponder a lustful thought, gossip behind someone's back, or any other such thing, then pray a quick prayer—"God, forgive me"— and move on about our day with little gratitude that such forgiveness cost the Son of God his very life.

Forgiveness does not mean that God looks down upon us and says, "It's okay what you have done; I'll just overlook it." No! To think that God merely overlooks sin is to completely misunderstand his holiness and righteousness. God can't overlook sin. Sin demands payment. Forgiveness demands payment. And the only death that was great enough, perfect enough, satisfying enough, to adequately and

---

1   Charles H. Spurgeon, "Redemption through Blood, the Gracious Forgiveness of Sins," in *The Metropolitan Tabernacle Pulpit* (Pasadena, TX: Pilgrim Publications, 1975), 37:304–305.

eternally pay this payment was the death of Jesus Christ.

The cross is the convergence of God's love and wrath. His great love for us is seen in his providing a substitute for us to bear the wrathful penalty due to our sin. Jesus takes our place. Stephen Charnock wrote,

> [Christ] received our evils to bestow his good and submitted to our curse to impart to us his blessings; sustained the extremity of that wrath we had deserved to confer upon us the grace he had purchased. The sin in us, which he was free from, was by divine estimation transferred upon him, as if he were guilty, that the righteousness he has, which we were destitute of, might be transferred upon us, as if we were innocent. He was made sin, as if he had sinned all the sins of men, and we were made righteousness, as if we had not sinned at all.[2]

Forgiveness by Faith

The only source of lasting forgiveness is God. We live in a culture that repeatedly implores us, "Forgive yourself." And

---

2 Stephen Charnock, "The Cleansing Virtue of Christ's Blood," in *Works*, 3:519.

while doing so may make you feel better about yourself for a few minutes, this quasi-spiritual slogan can never erase your guilt and shame. Only by faith, the Bible teaches, can we receive forgiveness. We aren't forgiven from sin because of virtues amassed, merits achieved, or even prayers prayed. Forgiveness only comes to those who by faith trust in Jesus Christ and his perfect work. We must come before God and cry out like the tax collector in Luke 18:13, "God, be merciful to me, a sinner!" Forgiveness comes "through faith in Jesus Christ for all who believe" (Rom. 3:22). In chapter 4 of Romans, Paul uses the faith of Abraham as our example, for he "grew strong in his faith as he gave glory to God, fully convinced that God was able to do what he had promised" (Rom. 4:20–21).

The joyful good news is that God is ready and quick to forgive. He doesn't reluctantly demonstrate his forgiveness but promises that if we confess our sins to him, he will undoubtedly forgive those sins (1 John 1:9). You may say, "I don't *feel* forgiven." The Bible never instructs us to base our forgiveness on the state of our emotions or how we feel at any given moment but on the concrete promises of God that if we confess, he will indeed forgive.

In a worshipful tone, John Owen wrote:

How many millions of sins in every one of the elect, every one of which is enough to condemn them all, hath this love overcome! What mountains of unbelief doth it remove! Look upon the conduct of any one saint, consider the frame of his heart, see the many stains and spots, the defilements and infirmities with which his life is contaminated, and tell me whether the love that bears with all this is not to be admired. And is not the same towards thousands every day? What streams of grace, purging, pardoning, quickening, assisting, do flow from it every day! This is our Beloved.[3]

Have you been forgiven? Does the guilt, misery, and shame of your sin haunt you? Do you feel hopeless? God will not simply overlook your sin, for he cannot. But in his great love, he has provided a substitute. He has provided One who took upon himself the wrath and penalty sin requires.

Even now, Jesus is ready to forgive you. He summons you

3   John Owen, *Of Communion with God the Father, Son, and Holy Ghost*, in *The Works of John Owen* (Edinburgh: The Banner of Truth Trust, 2009), 2:63.

to come to him in repentance and faith. Look to the cross of Christ, where he freely and willingly shed his precious blood in death to forgive sin.

SCRIPTURE

Psalm 103; Isaiah 43:22–25; Daniel 9:9; Ephesians 1:7–8; Hebrews 10:15–18

REFLECTION

1. What are believers saved from?
2. Why does forgiveness demand the shedding of blood?
3. What does the new covenant promise through Christ?
4. What should we base the assurance of our forgiveness upon?

5

Access

*Now in Christ Jesus you who once were far off
have been brought near by the blood of Christ.*

EPHESIANS 2:13

THERE'S NO BETTER PLACE WHERE WE CAN examine
and revel in the sufficiency of Christ on our behalf than in
the titles Scripture gives him. Throughout the New Testament, Jesus is known as:

- Cornerstone: "The stone which the builders rejected
  has become the cornerstone." (Matt. 21:42)
- Savior: "For unto you is born this day in the city of
  David a Savior, who is Christ the Lord." (Luke 2:11)

- Lamb of God: "The next day [John] saw Jesus coming toward him, and said, 'Behold, the Lamb of God, who takes away the sin of the world.'" (John 1:29)

- I Am: "Jesus said to them, 'Truly, truly, I say to you, before Abraham was, I am.'" (John 8:58)

- Good Shepherd: "I am the good shepherd. The good shepherd lays down his life for the sheep." (John 10:11)

- Head of the Church: "And he put all things under his feet and gave him as head over all things to the church." (Eph. 1:22)

- The Almighty: "Who is and who was and who is to come, the Almighty." (Rev. 1:8)

- King: "They will make war with the Lamb, and the Lamb will conquer them, because he is Lord of lords and King of kings." (Rev. 17:14)

- Alpha and Omega: "I am the Alpha and the Omega, the first and the last, the beginning and the end." (Rev. 22:13)

The list could go on and on, and within each of these titles is a reminder of our Lord's perfect work on behalf of his people.

There's another title for Christ so rich with meaning that we are sometimes in danger of forgetting it. This title extends back to the very beginning to encompass God's redemptive plan and extends forward into all eternity. That title is Jesus Christ as our High Priest.

There are multiple texts that grasp the depth and height of the implications of Jesus being our High Priest. For instance, we could look at our Lord's High Priestly Prayer in John 17, where, before his death, he intercedes in the upper room on behalf of all who will ever believe in his name. John 17 unveils for us the mediatorial work of Jesus as our High Priest who grants us access to God.

Left to ourselves, we have no inherent desire to approach God. Nothing within us longs or seeks for God. David is clear about this in Psalm 14:2–3:

> The LORD looks down from heaven
>   on the children of man,
>   to see if there are any who understand,
>   who seek after God.
> They have all turned aside;
>   together they have become corrupt;

there is none who does good,
not even one.

Apart from Christ, our Mediator, the sinner looks in vain for God. Perhaps you remember the story of the fall of Adam and Eve in Genesis 3. After eating the forbidden fruit, they fled from God in terror when they heard him walking in the garden. All men and women after our first parents do the same, because of sin.

Is there any access to God for fallen creatures such as us? The gospel's good news is a resounding *yes*, but only through an appointed Mediator. Jesus confirmed, "No one can come to me unless the Father who sent me draws him" (John 6:44).

Access to God is only possible through the mediatorial work of the Lord Jesus Christ—not through earthly priests, pastors, good works, or even angels—only Christ. Paul affirms this in Romans 5, saying, "Therefore, since we have been justified by faith, we have peace with God through our Lord Jesus Christ. Through him we have also obtained access by faith" (vv. 1–2).

Jesus Is Better

The first readers of the book of Hebrews were being threatened with severe persecution because of their faith in Christ, and discontentment began growing in their hearts as they were tempted to return to their past Jewish practices and rituals. Therefore, the writer of Hebrews put pen to parchment to reassert that Jesus' rightful place is one of absolute supremacy.

From the very first verses of chapter 1, the writer sets forth Christ as the one to whom the entire Old Testament points: "Long ago, at many times and in many ways, God spoke to our fathers by the prophets, but in these last days he has spoken to us by his Son, whom he appointed the heir of all things, through whom also he created the world" (Heb. 1:1–2). In subsequent chapters, he then sets Jesus forth as the *better way*:

Chapter 2: Jesus is better than angels.

Chapter 3: Jesus is better than Moses.

Chapters 4 and 5: Jesus is a better high priest.

Chapter 6: Jesus is the better fulfillment of God's promises.

Chapter 7: Jesus is the better guarantee of a better covenant.

Then, in verse 1 of chapter 8, the author of Hebrews presents his thesis: "Now the point in what we are saying is this... ." The main point, revealed in the mere thirteen verses of chapter 8, is that Jesus is an infinitely more sufficient priest who mediates a better covenant.

The weakness and imperfection of the priests of the tabernacle and temple in the Old Testament are evident in the fact that their job was never complete (Heb. 7:28). In their weakness, the Levites of the old covenant were able to enter the holy of holies to atone for the sins of the people one time each year. In stark contrast, Jesus has ascended into heaven, entered the heavenly temple of God's sanctuary, and been invited to sit down at "the right hand of the Majesty on high" (Heb. 1:3). The former priests' job was never finished—they never sat down—because the sacrifices they offered were never wholly sufficient. But when Christ offered the sacrifice of himself, he sat down, because his redemptive work had been perfectly accomplished. Remember the sweet words of our Lord on the cross: "It is finished" (John 19:30). Jesus became both the lamb slaughtered and the priest in one glorious self-sacrifice. He offers that sacrifice before God as the final reconciliation with God on behalf of his people, granting us access to God's throne.

The Jews reading Hebrews may have been reminded of the judicial practices of the ruling Sanhedrin, a council of seventy elders. Endowed with both religious and civil authority, when the council sat in judgment, the secretary on the left side of the judge was tasked with writing condemnations when the judge pronounced someone guilty. The secretary on the right wrote acquittals when someone was found innocent. As our Great High Priest, Jesus now resides upon the eternal seat of mercy, writing acquittals with his blood, fulfilling Hebrews 7:25: "He is able to save to the uttermost those who draw near to God through him, since he always lives to make intercession for them."

The promises of the new covenant in Jesus' blood are better. Jesus' blood is better than once-a-year atonement. Jesus' blood is better than earthly priests, golden lampstands, and incense. Jesus' blood accomplished the eternal redemption made by our High Priest, who was invited by God the Father to sit down at his right hand and carry on the work of intercession, granting us boldness as we approach the throne of grace.

John Bunyan challenges us to see Jesus—in his past work

of redemption and in his present ministry—as our High Priest. Rejoicing in our access, Bunyan writes,

Since Christ is an intercessor, I infer that believers should not rest at the cross for comfort; justification they should look for there, but being justified by his blood, they should ascend up after him to his throne. At the cross you will see him in his sorrows and humiliations, in his tears and blood; but follow him to where he is now, and then you shall see him in his robes—in his priestly robes and with his golden girdle about him. There you shall see him wearing the breastplate of judgment and with all your names written upon his heart. Then you shall perceive that the whole family in heaven and earth is named of him and how he prevails with God the Father of mercies for you. Stand still awhile and listen—yea, enter with boldness unto the holiest and see your Jesus as he now appears in the presence of God for you, what work he makes against the devil and sin and death and hell for you. Ah, it is brave following of Jesus Christ to the holiest. The veil is rent; you may see with open face as in a glass the glory of the Lord.[1]

Draw Near

Paul writes, "Now in Christ Jesus you who once were far off have been brought near by the blood of Christ" (Eph. 2:13). Notice the words "brought near." The idea here is of spiritual intimacy with God through Christ. Those who trust in the atoning work of Christ are freed from the penalty of sin, regenerated by the Holy Spirit, receive a new nature, are declared righteous, and are forgiven and cleansed "by the blood of Christ." And because of this, the new birth is "brought near" in experiencing spiritual intimacy, fellowship, and community with the triune God. Where there was once a barrier, there is now access. Where there was once fear, there is now boldness.

One of the most encouraging texts in all of the Bible is found in Hebrews 4:14–16:

Since then we have a great high priest who has passed through the heavens, Jesus, the Son of God, let us hold

---

1   John Bunyan, *Christ a Complete Saviour*, in *The Works of John Bunyan* (Edinburgh: The Banner of Truth Trust, 1999), 1:206.

fast our confession. For we do not have a high priest who is unable to sympathize with our weaknesses, but one who in every respect has been tempted as we are, yet without sin. Let us then with confidence draw near to the throne of grace, that we may receive mercy and find grace to help in time of need.

Here we have the implications of Jesus as our Great High Priest who bids us draw near to God. Do we take advantage of the tremendous access we have been granted? Paul says not only should we take advantage of it, but we should be bold in doing so: "We have boldness and access with confidence through our faith in him" (Eph. 3:12). God never says, "I don't have time for you now," or "Get your life straightened out and come back and see me." He is willing, ready, and desires intimate fellowship with his people. His gracious heart reaches out with countless invitations:

Come to me, all who labor and are heavy laden, and I will give you rest. (Matt. 11:28)

The Spirit and the Bride say, "Come." (Rev. 22:17)

What does it mean that we have access and can now draw near?

First, we draw near because we are weak. I think it's pretty clear by now in our varied descriptions of the horrible condition we are in as sinners that we don't have all the answers. Our sympathetic High Priest invites us to draw near and bring all of our weakness to him. We are never told to bear our burdens alone. David encourages us to "cast your burden on the LORD, and he will sustain you; he will never permit the righteous to be moved" (Ps. 55:22). Paul describes our access, "Do not be anxious about anything, but in everything by prayer and supplication with thanksgiving let your requests be made known to God" (Phil. 4:6). There is nothing God doesn't want to know about us. Take everything to him—weakness, burdens, cares, heartaches, problems, families, spouses, world events, lost car keys, decisions, finances, friendships, loved ones, sickness—*everything*.

Second, we draw near because we are powerless. How often do we think we can handle things in our families, churches, and lives? We falsely believe we have it all under control. However, all our good works will never advance us one inch closer to the throne of grace. Without Christ, we are utterly incapable and powerless to enter the presence of a holy God. When we don't recognize ourselves to be helpless and needy, we neglect prayer and communion with God. After Jesus ascended back to heaven, he sent the Holy Spirit and empowered his disciples to be his witnesses throughout the world (Acts 1:8). Without this divine power, we are useless.

Third, we draw near with confidence. There is no human priest we can gain access through, no mantra we must recite, no ritual we must endure. Instead, we draw near to the throne of God with confidence because the blood of our High Priest has given us access (Eph. 3:12). In ancient kingdoms, common people had no access to their rulers. Without permission, someone trying to approach the king's throne would likely be executed. Yet the Majesty of the cosmos invites all truly penitent, undeserving, and unfit people to his throne and promises mercy and grace (Heb. 4:16). Through Christ's perfect provision, righteous judgment has been diverted, and we now receive grace. When do we come to God? Now. "Behold, now is the favorable time; behold, now is the day of salvation" (2 Cor. 6:2).

When your whole life seems to be coming apart at the

seams, you feel discontented with your circumstances, you feel like your ministry is falling apart, and even that your family is unraveling, you can cry for help. Our Great High Priest takes you by the hand and ushers you before the throne of your Father, and he freely and lovingly lavishes his abundant mercy and grace upon you. What more could you want?

SCRIPTURE

Psalm 55:22; John 17; Ephesians 2:13; Hebrews 1:1–2; Hebrews 4:14–16

REFLECTION

1. Why is it so vitally necessary that Jesus serve as our High Priest?
2. What is Christ's present ministry on behalf of believers, and why is it important?
3. What are some implications of Jesus serving as our High Priest?
4. Since we now, through Christ, have access to God, list some practical ways in which you can draw near to God.

6

Justification

Since, therefore, we have now been justified
by his blood, much more shall we be
saved by him from the wrath of God.

ROMANS 5:9

OVER THE PAST SEVERAL CHAPTERS, we've defined and examined man's sinful condition as revealed in Scripture. The conclusion has been stark but honest: human beings are not only a mess; we are spiritually dead. We are incapable of doing anything to rescue ourselves from the bondage in which we are born. Apart from Christ's sacrifical blood and the Holy Spirit's gracious intervention, we are slaves of sin and love it.

In Ephesians 2, Paul vividly describes our position before the Lord Jesus Christ:

> And you were dead in the trespasses and sins in which you once walked, following the course of this world, following the prince of the power of the air, the spirit that is now at work in the sons of disobedience— among whom we all once lived in the passions of our flesh, carrying out the desires of the body and the mind, and were by nature children of wrath, like the rest of mankind. (Eph. 2:1–3)

Sin has rendered us incapable of pleasing God. We remain dead in our sin despite our good works, philanthropic efforts, or meritorious deeds. If we were left in the opening verses of Ephesians 2, we would be of all people most miserable, but Paul adds, "But God …" in verse 4. If not for these words, we would be hopeless. He continues,

> But God, being rich in mercy, because of the great love with which he loved us, even when we were dead in our trespasses, made us alive together with Christ—by

grace you have been saved—and raised us up with him and seated us with him in the heavenly places in Christ Jesus, so that in the coming ages he might show the immeasurable riches of his grace in kindness toward us in Christ Jesus. For by grace you have been saved through faith. And this is not your own doing; it is the gift of God, not a result of works, so that no one may boast. For we are his workmanship, created in Christ Jesus for good works, which God prepared beforehand, that we should walk in them. (Eph. 2:4–10)

God extends his "rich ... mercy" and "great love" to bring us "together with Christ." God fuses us with Christ. This is what theologians refer to as union with Christ. Jesus serves as our representative head through his birth, life, death, burial, resurrection, and ascension. Believers are so united with Christ that we become beneficiaries of his substitutionary work of salvation.

The effect of this union is the free gift of justification, whereby God declares believers to be righteous, regenerating them to new life, granting repentance and faith, and declaring them forgiven and accepted before him. He is the vine, and we are the branches (see John 15:1–11).

Relationship with God

We often talk of our "relationship with God." In our evangelistic efforts, we ask people, "Do you have a relationship with God?" The most common answer is, "I've done this," or "I've achieved that." Sinners wrongly believe that the merits of their self-righteousness will bring them into a right relationship with God. According to Paul, nothing could be further from the truth, for our standing before God is "not a result of works, so that no one may boast" (Eph. 2:9). Only justification offers the correct answer as to how depraved sinners come into a right relationship with a holy God.

Jesus clarifies that our supposed good works aren't enough to make us righteous. Jesus surprisingly said in Matthew 5:48, "You therefore must be perfect, as your heavenly Father is perfect." Perfect?! How is that possible? In other words, if you would be right before God, if God would accept you, you don't need goodness or merit or works; you need perfection. Jesus is clear: perfection is the prerequisite for a right relationship with God.

Salvation isn't complicated—you simply must be as

perfect as God. This leads us back to the question, how is perfection possible? Well, it isn't. Left with our countless endeavors and good works to achieve perfection, salvation is impossible, and we are left condemned in our sin.

The only way human beings can enter a right relationship with God and be saved is to be given external righteousness. Theologians call this an alien righteousness, meaning it comes to us from God alone. The beauty of the gospel is that God provides what he requires in the person and work of his only begotten Son, the Lord Jesus Christ. Justification lies at the very heart of the gospel. J. I. Packer describes the vital role of justification in the gospel: "The gospel centers upon justification; that is, upon remission of sins and acceptance of our persons that goes with it."[1]

The gospel involves the incarnation, crucifixion, and resurrection of Christ. These are events that happened during a specific time in history. But the gospel isn't merely a set of historical facts. The gospel extends beyond time and place to how what Jesus accomplished is appropriated to sinners—how we can be saved. The gospel would not be good

---

1   J. I. Packer, *Knowing God*, 151.

news unless it includes *how* we come into union with Christ and *how* he becomes our Savior.

While other religions in the world are based on personal merit, Christianity is the only religion based on what has been done *for* us instead of what we have done. God welcomes those who believe based solely on the righteousness of Christ, which he graciously and mercifully lavishes upon those who come to him by faith alone. As Paul affirms, "To the one who does not work but believes in him who justifies the ungodly, his faith is counted as righteousness" (Rom. 4:5).

Therefore, justification is defined as an instantaneous, gracious, and merciful act of God whereby he imputes the perfect and full righteousness of Jesus Christ to the believer's account, by faith alone, and legally declares him or her to be perfectly righteousness, forgiven of all sin, free from condemnation, and wholly acceptable in his sight.

Now, let's unpack this.

Christ, Our Substitute

Does God just dismiss our sin and count us righteous? To ask more precisely: Since we stand guilty before God condemned in our sin, how can a holy God remain just and still justify the ungodly?

In our definition of justification, notice the word *impute* or *imputation*. The answer to the questions above is found in the doctrine of imputation—unrighteous sinners are declared, counted, or credited the perfect righteousness of Christ solely based on his perfect work. In short, Christ takes our place. On the cross, Christ becomes our substitute and freely takes upon himself the penalty for sin that we deserve and pays what we owe with his own blood. In turn, we are imputed with his righteousness and granted eternal life.

God imputes our sin to Christ

In 2 Corinthians 5:21, Paul states, "For our sake [God the Father] made [Christ the Son] to be sin who knew no sin." On the cross, God the Father counted Jesus as having committed all the sins of all those who would ever believe in him. Jesus did not become a sinner on the cross. To even consider such a concept is blasphemous. Instead, God judicially reckoned Christ to have committed the sins of those for whom he died. Peter explains, "He himself bore our sins in his body on the tree, that we might die to sin and live to righteousness. By his wounds you have been healed" (1 Pet. 2:24; cf. Isa. 53:4–6). If you are a believer, Jesus was seen by the Father on the cross as having committed every sin you have ever committed or will ever commit. Only because Jesus has become our substitute are we forgiven and justified.

God imputes Christ's righteousness to believers

It is not enough to be counted as sinless. That's only one side of the gospel equation. We must also be counted as righteous. Therefore, justification is a two-fold imputation.

Not only is Christ imputed with our sin on the cross, but, in turn, we are imputed with his perfect righteousness. Through the blood of Christ, not only does he pay the penalty we deserve, but he also grants us the righteousness we do not deserve. Just as our sins are reckoned to his account, his perfect righteousness is reckoned to ours.

Paul makes clear in Romans 5:9 that it is "by his blood" that we are justified. The blood of Christ is the conduit through which God imputes our sin to Christ and imputes his righteousness to us. Recall the words of Hebrews 9:22:

"Without the shedding of blood there is no forgiveness of sins."

In every way possible, Christ becomes our substitute. He lived a perfect, obedient life we must live. He dies a perfect, atoning death we must die. An eternity of good works would never achieve the perfect righteousness God requires, yet Jesus freely offers to all who believe.

Paul encapsulates this glorious truth in Romans 5:17:

For if, because of one man's trespass, death reigned through that one man, much more will those who receive the abundance of grace and the free gift of righteousness reign in life through the one man Jesus Christ.

Faith Alone

Perhaps you are now wondering how you can be justified and have the perfect righteousness of Christ. Maybe you're asking, how can what Christ accomplished on the cross two thousand years ago be applied to me?

By faith alone.

Faith unites us to Christ in his perfectly obedient life,

death, and resurrection, so that his punishment counts for our punishment and his righteousness counts for our righteousness.[2] Paul said in Romans 4:5, "To the one who does not work but believes in him who justifies the ungodly, his faith is counted as righteousness." We are righteous not just by faith but by faith *alone*. Salvation came to the thief on the cross not because of any good work he had done but in the mere evidence of his faith (Luke 23:43).

Faith in Christ and his finished work on the cross and resurrection is the means through which we receive righteousness. Lest we believe that we contribute anything to our salvation, Paul clarifies that even our faith is a gift from God (Eph. 2:8). Therefore, faith is the means of our salvation, not its ground.

In seasons of doubt, don't look to your faith for assurance of salvation; look to Christ. Faith doesn't earn righteousness; for that we look to Christ. Nothing in salvation is of our own doing or merit, for if it were, you would not truly have *salvation*.

Scripture bids us come to Christ with empty hands. As

---

2   John MacArthur, *Essential Christian Doctrine* (Wheaton, IL: Crossway Books, 2021), 331.

the old hymn reminds us:

Nothing in my hand I bring,
  Simply to the cross I cling;
Naked, come to thee for dress;
  Helpless, look to thee for grace;
Foul, I to the fountain fly;
  Wash me, Savior, or I die.[3]

We have no hope apart from Christ. We have no salvation apart from Christ. We have no righteousness apart from Christ. This is why the doctrine of justification is vital in the gospel message. Only because our sin has been imputed to Christ and his righteousness imputed to us are we declared just and do we enter a right relationship with a holy God. John 3:16 is the resounding anthem for all those in union with Christ: "For God so loved the world, that he gave his only Son, that whoever believes in him should not perish but have eternal life."

3   Augustus Toplady, "Rock of Ages, Cleft for Me" (1776).

SCRIPTURE

John 15:1–11; Romans 5:17; Ephesians 2:1–10

REFLECTION

1. Define the doctrine of justification.
2. Why aren't our good works sufficient to make us righteous?
3. How does our understanding of imputation affect what we believe about justification?
4. Why must faith be a gift from God?

7

Sanctification

*So Jesus also suffered outside the gate in order to
sanctify the people through his own blood.*

HEBREWS 13:12

THE GOSPEL INVOLVES BOTH JUSTIFICATION and
sanctification. You can't have one without the other, as they
are inseparably linked. Just like justification, sanctification
is a gospel work, and both deal with sin in the life of the
believer. While justification is an instantaneous one-time
event whereby God brings us into a right legal standing
before him by dealing with the penalty of our sin through
Christ, sanctification is a progressive work of shaping us by
the Holy Spirit into the image of Christ by dealing with the

dominion of sin in our lives.

Justification is a declaration that a sinner is righteous through the finished work of Christ. Sanctification is the transformation of the sinner in righteousness through the continued work of Christ by the Holy Spirit.

Our standing before God is a finished act. Justification ensures that believers will never stand before God again condemned in the guilt of their sin. Believers will never again stand before God condemned in the guilt of their sin, because Christ took upon himself that wrath and stood in our place that we might have his righteousness imputed to our account. Sanctification ensures that we are now alive to righteousness and begin the long, progressive journey to become like Christ by obeying his commands, producing the fruit of the Holy Spirit, and actively putting sin to death.

To put it simply, justification renders us dead to sin while sanctification demands that we put sin to death (Rom. 6:1–23; 8:1–11). The same faith placed in Christ at justification is now actively pursuing Christ in sanctification.

"From one degree of glory to another"
Any believer who has been a believer for any length of time

would be the first to confess that the Christian life is difficult. Living in a fallen, sinful, and hostile world is a struggle. This should never come as a shock to us. In fact, Jesus warned us that "in the world you will have tribulation." Lest we despair, Jesus continues, "Take heart, I have overcome the world" (John 16:33). Sanctification involves "looking to Jesus, the founder and perfecter of our faith, who for the joy that was set before him endured the cross, despising the shame, and is seated at the right hand of the throne of God" (Heb. 12:2).

Therefore, the Christian life is the progressive *looking* to Jesus, who then transforms us "into the same image from one degree of glory to another" (2 Cor. 3:18). This is the heart of sanctification: looking so intently at the glory of Christ that we are transformed into his image. And this process continues for the rest of our Christian walk. Paul echoed this desire in his own life: "Forgetting what lies behind and straining forward to what lies ahead, I press on toward the goal for the prize of the upward call of God in Christ Jesus" (Phil. 3:13–14).

In 2 Corinthians, as Paul was experiencing tremendous difficulties in pastoral ministry, he emphasized the dichotomy of being free from sin yet daily dying to sin. He wrote to the believers in Corinth, "We do not lose heart. Though our outer self is wasting away, our inner self is being renewed day by day. For this light momentary affliction is preparing for us an eternal weight of glory beyond all comparison" (2 Cor. 4:16–17). Paul recognized that we face the inevitable war between our old flesh ("outer self") and our new regenerated spirit ("inner self"). These two will be in constant conflict with one another. Similarly, Paul encourages the Colossians to "put on the new self, which is being renewed in knowledge after the image of its creator" (Col. 3:10). The goal of sanctification is increased likeness to Christ. We would call this *holiness*, "without which no one will see the Lord" (Heb. 12:14).

Paul implores the Ephesian Christians to "walk in a manner worthy of the calling to which you have been called" (Eph. 4:1). This isn't a suggestion. He states at the beginning of verse 1, "I ... urge you." Paul understands the urgency. The metaphor of *walking* appears throughout Paul's instructions and points to an urgency in the Christian life. Sanctification is our obedience in the gospel—you who once *walked* in transgressions and sins (Eph. 2:1–2)—you now must *walk* in the good works God has intended for you (Eph. 2:10). Believers should not continue to live in the sin from which they were rescued. The whole New Testament is filled with verses of instruction regarding how we grow in holiness and are sanctified in heart, word, affection, and deed.

A Trinitarian Masterpiece

The process of sanctification is a work of the Father, Son, and Holy Spirit. Each member of the eternal Godhead is involved in making believers more holy.

Sanctification is predominantly a work of God the Father. Paul said, "Now may the God of peace himself sanctify you completely, and may your whole spirit and soul and body be kept blameless at the coming of our Lord Jesus Christ" (1 Thess. 5:23). It is God's sanctifying purpose in our lives—drawing us to himself, giving us his Word, revealing his will, granting power to kill sin—that makes us increasingly like Christ.

Jesus Christ secures our sanctification both positionally and progressively. The writer of Hebrews reminds us that our positional sanctification is only made possible through Christ's blood (Heb. 13:12). Through his finished work on the cross and union with him, Christ positionally sets us before his Father as perfectly holy. But he also progressively sanctifies us by setting before us the standard and example toward which we should strive. We're reminded that God sent Christ to be our "wisdom from God, righteousness and sanctification and redemption" (1 Cor. 1:30). Jesus is the standard and example we are to emulate in our Christian walk (1 Pet. 2:21). Back to the metaphor of walking, John says, "Whoever says he abides in him ought to walk in the same way in which he walked" (1 John 2:6).

Jesus doesn't leave us to fumble about in the darkness of this world trying to figure out how to sanctify ourselves on our own. Quite the contrary. Jesus promised to send the Holy Spirit to be our Helper (John 14:6, 26; 15:26; 16:7). Peter talks of the "sanctification of the Spirit, for obedience to Jesus Christ and for sprinkling with his blood" (1 Pet. 1:2). At the moment of our salvation, the Holy Spirit takes up residence in our lives in order to make us like Jesus. He achieves this by producing within us the "fruit of the Spirit" (Gal. 5:22). The Christian life would be impossible to live apart from the animating, helping, and beautifying work of the Spirit.

In his book *Transforming Grace*, Jerry Bridges helps us to understand the juxtaposition between positional and progressive sanctification and the role the Trinity plays in each:

Initial sanctification occurs instantly at the moment of salvation when we are delivered from the kingdom of darkness and brought into the Kingdom of Christ (see Colossians 1:13). Progressive sanctification continues over time until we go to be with the Lord. Initial sanctification is entirely the work of God the Holy Spirit who imparts to us the very life of Christ. Progressive sanctification is also the work of the Holy Spirit, but it involves a response on our part so that we as believers are actively involved in the process.[1]

Passive and Active

"What am I to do?" you may ask. Do we play any role whatsoever in the cultivation of holiness without our lives? After all, it's the blood of Christ that secures our sanctification. It's the Father who makes us blameless, the Son who declares it

---

1   Jerry Bridges, *Transforming Grace* (Colorado Springs, CO: NavPress, 1991), 112–113.

so, and the Spirit who produces fruit.

Theologians recognize a dual aspect to sanctification—passive and active. Sanctification is *passive* in that, positionally, it is a finished work before God as we depend totally upon him to sanctify us. Sanctification is also *active* in that we decide to walk obediently, putting sin to death and striving to conform our lives to Christ.

To describe sanctification as passive in no way entails that we can sit back, grow lazy, and wait for God to make us holy without actively pursuing holiness. The passive aspect of sanctification simply means that we are dependent upon God to ultimately make us holy, that we pray for him to do whatever is necessary to make us holy, and that we willingly submit to his will to achieve what he desires in our lives. Paul entreats us to "present your bodies as a living sacrifice, holy and acceptable to God, which is your spiritual worship" (Rom. 12:1).

To define sanctification as active doesn't mean that it's completely left up to us. Paul reminds us to "work out your own salvation with fear and trembling" (Phil. 2:12). Focusing again on our metaphor of walking, notice these commands directed to believers:

- "Walk by faith, not by sight" (2 Cor. 5:7).
- "Walk by the Spirit, and you will not gratify the desires of the flesh" (Gal. 5:16).
- "Walk in love" (Eph. 5:2).
- "Walk as children of light" (Eph. 5:8).
- "Walk in a manner worthy of the Lord" (Col. 1:10).
- "Walk in him" (Col. 2:6).
- "Walk properly before outsiders" (1 Thess. 4:12).

The Spirit isn't commanded to walk; believers are. "Walking," for Paul, is shorthand for practical Christian living—living out what has been planted within. Paul bridges this gap between passive and active in Romans 8:13: "If *by the Spirit you put to death* the deeds of the body, you will live." The Spirit animates us to put to death the deeds of the body, but *we* are commanded to do so. We aren't robots. The Spirit provides the power, and we use that power to obey Christ.

We are saved to be made holy. We are made holy in the blood of Christ, his imputed righteousness, and union with him. God now spends the rest of our days making us holy through Christ, molding us into his image, helping us kill sin, and changing our affections. We are being made blameless (Col. 1:22).

We are made blameless through means. As I already stated, we don't approach the Christian life lackadaisically, exerting no effort whatsoever toward growth in holiness. God uses means to make us holy. God uses his Word, revealed in the Bible, as instructions to illuminate our path to holiness. God uses prayer as the means through which we bring out requests, temptations, and struggles before him. In response to our sin, God uses discipline to constantly remind us of the direction in which we are to walk.

Regarding God's employment of means in our sanctification, I leave you with the words of J. C. Ryle:

When I speak of "means," I have in view Bible-reading, private prayer, regular attendance on public worship, regular hearing of God's Word, and regular reception of the Lord's Supper. I lay it down as a simple matter of fact, that no one who is careless about such things must ever expect to make much progress in sanctification. I can find no record of any eminent saint who ever neglected them. They are appointed channels through which the Holy Spirit conveys fresh supplies of grace to the soul, and strengthens the work which He has begun in the inward man. Let men call this legal doctrine if they please, but I will never shrink from declaring my belief that there are no "spiritual gains without pains." Our God is a God who works by means, and He will never bless the soul of that man who pretends to be so high and spiritual that he can get on without them.[2]

SCRIPTURE

Romans 6:1–23; 2 Corinthians 4:16–17; Galatians 5:22–23; Philippians 2:12–13

REFLECTION

1. How is justification different from sanctification?
2. Why is sanctification described as *progressive*?
3. How is sanctification both positional and progressive?
4. Describe the primary role each member of the Trinity—Father, Son, and Holy Spirit—plays in our justification and sanctification.

---

2   J. C. Ryle, *Holiness* (Chicago, IL: Moody Publishers, 2010), 54–55.

8

Glorification

And those whom he predestined he also called,
and those whom he called he also justified, and
those whom he justified he also glorified.

ROMANS 8:30

LIFE, EVEN THE CHRISTIAN LIFE, is fraught with "good-byes." From friends parting ways after a sweet reunion to sitting bedside when a believer takes their last breath, even Christians, like all human beings, face unavoidable sorrow. However, we do "not grieve as others do who have not hope" (1 Thess. 4:13). Our hope acts as a buttress supporting the weight of our sometimes-heavy sorrow.

Hope is only possible in the Christian life because of our

new birth in Christ—union with his death and resurrection. The apostle Peter rejoices in this redemptive hope: "Blessed be the God and Father of our Lord Jesus Christ! According to his great mercy, he has caused us to be born again to a *living hope* through the resurrection of Jesus Christ from the dead" (1 Pet. 1:3).

The foundation of our *living hope* is the resurrection of Jesus Christ. Because he lives, we too shall live (John 14:19). Outside of knowing Christ, there is no hope (Eph. 2:12). William Gurnall points to the exclusivity of the believer's hope: "True hope is a jewel that no one wears but Christ's bride, a grace with which no one is graced but the believer's soul."[1]

Hope is inseparably linked to faith: "Faith is the assurance of things hoped for, the conviction of things not seen" (Heb. 11:1). Gurnall observed the interconnectedness of faith and hope by defining hope as a love letter from God:

Who goes out to meet him whom he believes will not come? The promise is, as it were, God's love letter to

1   William Gurnall, *The Christian in Complete Armor* (Edinburgh: The Banner of Truth Trust, 2002), 515.

his church and spouse in which he opens his very heart and tells all he means to do for her. Faith reads and embraces it with joy, whereupon the believing soul, by hope, looks out of this window with a longing expectation to see her husband's [presence] come in the accomplishment thereof.[2]

Faith embraces the promises, and hope looks with anticipation. In concert together, faith and hope undergird every obstacle we face so that we may "rejoice in hope of the glory of God" (Rom. 5:2). Our hope reaches in faith for what we do not yet fully possess—glorification.[3] Puritan William Ames wrote: "The first degree of this glorification begun is the apprehension and sense of the love of God shining forth in Christ upon the communion which the faithful have with him (Rom. 5:5), the love of God issued abroad in our hearts by the Holy Spirit given to us."[4]

The glorification for which we long as believers is planted

2   William Gurnall, *The Christian in Complete Armor*, 515.
3   Joel R. Beeke and Paul M. Smalley, *Reformed Systematic Theology: Spirit and Salvation* (Wheaton, IL: Crossway Books, 2021), 1016.
4   William Ames, *Marrow of Sacred Divinity* (London: Edward Griffen for Henry Overton, 1642), 147.

without our hearts at salvation by the Holy Spirit through the blood of Christ. Ames references Romans 5:5, which links our hope and salvation: "Hope does not put us to shame, because God's love has been poured into our hearts through the Holy Spirit who has been given to us." Hope longs for, prays for, and groans for glorification.

The Final Link

Justification and sanctification are not the final links in the golden chain of salvation. The benefits of the blood of Christ shed on our behalf extend beyond justifying and sanctifying. Paul wrote, "Those whom he justified *he also glorified*" (Rom. 8:30). The implication is that God isn't finished with the justified. Salvation only begins with justification. In other words, our salvation is not yet complete. Believers have been declared righteous in Christ, had the penalty of their sin paid, been indwelt by the Holy Spirit, and are now being sanctified into the image of Christ, but God isn't done with us until we are glorified with him.

Justification is a past act when God instantaneously declares us righteous by imputing our sin to Christ and his righteousness to us. In essence, like the Israelites applied the blood to their doorposts in Egypt, Christ applies his sufficient atoning blood to our account. Once we have been saved from the penalty and power of sin, sanctification is a process whereby the Holy Spirit makes us increasingly like Christ to finally free us from the presence of sin when we die and enter the Lord's presence.

But this isn't the end. Paul promises, "When Christ who is your life appears, then you also will appear with him in glory" (Col. 3:4). In the final resurrection, the final link to our salvation will be complete, for "when he appears we shall be like him, because we shall see him as he is" (1 John 3:2).

New Bodies

Paul describes our inward groaning as we anticipate our blessed hope of glory: "We ourselves, who have the first-fruits of the Spirit, groan inwardly as we wait eagerly for adoption as sons, the redemption of our bodies" (Rom. 8:23). Notice the final words of this verse, "the redemption of our *bodies*." At death, the believer enters the presence of God wholly sanctified, awaiting the final resurrection, but without a body. Glorification involves a new body that all believers will receive simultaneously when Christ returns. William Ames describes this blessed event:

Perfect glorification takes away all imperfection from soul and body and communication of all perfection. This is granted to the soul immediately after the separation of it from the body (2 Cor. 5:2; Phil. 1:23; Heb. 12:23). But it is not ordinarily granted to the soul and body jointly before the last day, wherein all the faithful shall be perfected together in Christ (Eph. 4:13; Phil. 3:20–21).[5]

This is our guaranteed hope (Eph. 1:13–14). Paul urges us to look beyond this transitory world in which we live to the glory that awaits us in Christ: "But our citizenship is in heaven, and from it we await a Savior, the Lord Jesus Christ, who will transform our lowly body to be like his glorious body, by the power that enables him even to subject all things to himself" (Phil. 3:20–21). The hope of glorification is freedom in both body and soul, not just from the

5   William Ames, *Marrow of Sacred Divinity*, 150.

power of sin but from the presence of sin. Ames called it "perfect glorification." In other words, this is the moment our salvation is complete. This is the "prize of the upward call of God in Christ Jesus" that Paul so vehemently pressed toward—being made like Jesus (Phil. 3:14). Hope longs for, prays for, groans for, and presses for glorification.

Since justification perfected our soul in righteousness, glorification primarily involves our body. What will our bodies be like? We must look to Christ. Jesus' glorified resurrected body is the exact image of our glorified resurrection body. Jesus wasn't a ghost or mystical spirit that emerged from the tomb. Instead, he had a physical body, the same physical body that three days earlier had died on the cross. After his resurrection, Jesus was just as human as he was before his resurrection. He declared the physical nature of his body when he invited his disciples to touch him: "See my hands and my feet, that it is I myself. Touch me, and see. For a spirit does not have flesh and bones as you see that I have" (Luke 24:39).

From Thomas touching Jesus to Jesus eating breakfast with his disciples on the shore of the Sea of Galilee, the evidence is clear that Jesus' body was an actual physical body.

Therefore, to say that we will be like Christ is to indicate that our glorified bodies will also be physical. Paul teaches this very truth in 2 Corinthians 5:1–4:

> For we know that if the tent that is our earthly home is destroyed, we have a building from God, a house not made with hands, eternal in the heavens. For in this tent we groan, longing to put on our heavenly dwelling, if indeed by putting it on we may not be found naked. For while we are still in this tent, we groan, being burdened—not that we would be unclothed, but that we would be further clothed, so that what is mortal may be swallowed up by life.

Paul uses the metaphor of a house to teach us what will occur to our bodies at the final resurrection. While justified believers currently dwell in a physical body, an "earthly tent," we fervently await the day when we will "put on our heavenly dwelling," which is also physical. In Romans 8:21–23, Paul defines glorification, as I stated earlier, as "the redemption of our *bodies*." We aren't going to receive a brand-new body by discarding the old, but our current bodies will be redeemed, that is, made new—glorified.

In our glorified state, our bodies will not have the same limitations that they had when subjected to the curse of sin. Our glorified bodies will never experience hunger, fatigue, disease, age, injury, stress, weakness, depression, heartache, suffering, or limitation. Instead, they will mirror Christ perfectly in power and glory. Matthew 13:43 states that "the righteous will shine like the sun in the kingdom of their Father." Our glorified bodies will so perfectly reflect the radiance and majesty of Christ that they will mirror forth in the eternal kingdom as the sun.

Freedom from Sin

As glorious as freedom from physical infirmities will be, it pales in comparison to eternal freedom from the curse of sin. Never knowing a world free from sin's curse, we are incapable of even conceiving of a universe and body free from sin's presence. "Glorification," according to Ames, "is a real transmutation [i.e., transformation] of a man from misery or the punishment of sin unto happiness eternal."[6] As

---

6   William Ames, *Marrow of Sacred Divinity*, 146.

sin mars our happiness and joy, the absence of sin will allow our happiness and joy to fully express itself in unimaginable ways as we eternally worship and adore God unhindered by sin.

Whereas the process of sanctification is sometimes a struggle and fight against the sin of our former nature without Christ, glorification will know no such struggle or fight. The promise of Revelation 21:27 is that the eternal kingdom will be completely free from sin, temptation, or its consequences: "Nothing unclean will ever enter it, nor anyone who does what is detestable or false, but only those who are written in the Lamb's book of life." Only the glorified will experience the exhilaration of being entirely and irreversibly free from sin.

All because of and through the blood of the Lamb.

Hope isn't some nebulous abstraction based on false claims. Paul said, if we "have hope in this life only, we are of all people most to be pitied" (1 Cor. 15:19). The foundation of our *living hope* is the resurrection of Jesus Christ, through which his people are promised resurrected glorification, new bodies like his, and freedom from the presence of sin.

Rejoice, saints, that your hope is anchored in God's

promises to bring us home to himself.

SCRIPTURE

Romans 8:26–30; 1 Corinthians 15:19;
Philippians 3:12–21; 1 Peter 1:3

REFLECTION

1. What is the believer's ultimate hope?
2. What happens when our salvation is finally completed?
3. How does God make us like Jesus?
4. What will our glorified bodies be like?

9

Victory

Thanks be to God, who gives us the
victory through our Lord Jesus Christ.

1 CORINTHIANS 15:57

REDEMPTION, PROPITIATION, CLEANSING, forgiveness,
access, justification, sanctification, glorification—like individual notes on a sheet of music, these words weave together
a crescendo of praise to the Christ who atones. As believers,
our lives are constantly lived *coram Deo* (before the face of
God) in the harmony of this theological orchestra.

Paul echoes this praise in 1 Corinthians 15:57: "Thanks
be to God, who gives us the victory through our Lord
Jesus Christ." 1 Corinthians 15 is Paul's sweeping narrative

exposition of Jesus' triumph over death, hell, and the grave and of how the same power is appropriated to all who are under the blood of Christ. Because of Christ's atonement on the cross and resurrection from the dead, all who are in union with him, cleansed and forgiven from their sin and having been justified by his grace, can look death squarely in the eyes and confidently ask:

O death, where is your victory?
O death, where is your sting? (v. 55)

Paul transitions to the promise of victory in this chapter. Without Christ, death has victory over us because we are born enslaved to sin. Death has lost its power in Christ, and we now have "victory through our Lord Jesus Christ." The same power that raised Jesus from the grave is the same power now dwelling in all believers, empowering them to faithfully live out the very gospel that has been born within. That which we are incapable of doing for ourselves God has accomplished for us and in us "through our Lord Jesus Christ."

On our behalf, Jesus stepped down from his glory, took

on flesh, lived a sinlessly obedient life, fulfilled every command of God's law, joyfully submitted himself to death upon a cross, removed our sin by paying the penalty we owed, stood in our place condemned before God, satisfied every requirement for our redemption, forgave and justified us from the curse of the law, conquered death, raised from the dead, and is now seated at the Father's right hand in glory. Jesus is our Victor, and this victory he accomplished for us he now freely gives to us. Christ stood condemned to provide us with victory. "Christ redeemed us from the curse of the law by becoming a curse for us" (Gal. 3:13).

In doxological gratitude for all Christ has done for us, Isaac Ambrose reflects, "Let us joy in Jesus… . Hath he drunk all the cup of God's wrath and left none for us? How should we be but cheered? Precious souls! Why are you afraid? There is no death, no hell, 'no condemnation to them that are in Christ Jesus' (Rom. 8:1)."[1]

How Can It Be?

Eighteenth-century hymn writer Charles Wesley often

---

1   Ambrose, "Looking unto Jesus," 400.

found himself lost in wonder, love, and praise as he meditated on the atonement of Christ. One such meditation asks the simple question, "How can it be?"

> And can it be that I should gain
>   An int'rest in the Savior's blood?
> Died He for me, who caused His pain?
>   For me, who Him to death pursued?
> Amazing love! how can it be
>   That Thou, my God, shouldst die for me?
> Amazing love! how can it be
>   That Thou, my God, shouldst die for me?[2]

In our study together, we've examined this "Amazing love!" by exploring a few of the inexhaustible benefits of the atonement of Christ. "But," you might respond, "I still struggle with temptation and sin." While it is true to say that the blood of Christ perfectly and eternally cleanses us from all sin, we also confess that Christ's blood keeps on cleansing us of sin. Until glorification, we are not free from

---

2   Charles Wesley, "And Can It Be, That I Should Gain?" (1738).

the presence of sin or the inward groaning to be free from our flesh (Rom. 8:22–23).

Victory is ours eternally through Christ from the consequences of sin, and victory is ours daily through Christ from the power of sin. This victory is possible only through the blood drawn from Immanuel's veins. As we seek to live in Christ's victory faithfully, we must realize that the same blood required to forgive and cleanse from sin is the same blood necessary to promote a life of holiness. How does this happen?

First, the blood of Christ reminds us to enjoy our "no condemnation" status before God. The atoning blood of Christ sets us free from the condemnation in which we once stood. During Israel's captivity in Egypt, the death angel visited anyone who did not have the blood of the Passover lamb applied to the doorpost of his home. Sacrificial blood was necessary in order to avoid falling under the condemnation of God. Likewise, today, all who do not have the blood of Christ applied to their hearts by faith stand condemned before God in their sin. But all those who have had their sins washed in the Lamb's blood stand victorious in Christ before the throne of God. Paul affirmed, "There is therefore now no condemnation for those who are in Christ Jesus" (Rom. 8:1). Because of the blood of Christ, you are no longer under the wrath of God.

Second, the blood of Christ reminds us of our reconciled relationship with God. The blood of Christ has brought us into a right relationship with God. We were once alienated from God—strangers and foreigners. Paul describes unbelievers in Ephesians 4:18 as "darkened in their understanding, alienated from the life of God because of the ignorance that is in them, due to their hardness of heart." Christ reverses this alienation and reconciles us to God (Rom. 5:10; 2 Cor. 5:18). Where we were once forbidden, we now have access. "For through [Christ] we ... have access in one Spirit to the Father. So then you are no longer strangers and aliens, but you are fellow citizens with the saints and members of the household of God" (Eph. 2:18–19). While we are strangers, God is under no obligation to hear or answer our prayers. But as his children, God longs for our fellowship in prayer and desires that we bring all of our petitions before him.

Third, the blood of Christ reminds us to cry out to God for help. In Jesus' first pronouncement of blessing in his Sermon on the Mount, he says, "Blessed are the poor in spirit, for theirs is the kingdom of heaven" (Matt. 5:3). The word "poor" means to have a beggarly spirit—to be keenly aware that they are spiritually impoverished and must rely exclusively on God's grace for salvation and all of life. The sufficiency of the blood of Christ reminds us that we are entirely reliant upon God's grace both in salvation and to meet all our needs.

In complete dependence upon God's undeserved kindness, David cried, "Incline your ear, O LORD, and answer me, for I am poor and needy" (Ps. 86:1). Apart from the kindness of the Lord, David lacked spiritual ability. The blood of Christ reminds us that we are "poor in spirit" and bankrupt of this world. Do you feel spiritually inadequate? Are you afraid to approach God—yet again—with your neediness? Never fear! Our heavenly Father stands ready and waiting with open arms to receive his beloved children who have nothing to plead but the blood of Christ. Cry out to him, "Nothing in my hand I bring; simply to the cross I cling."

Fourth, the blood of Christ reminds us to mourn over our present sin. As I've already stated, believers are never entirely free from sin until we lay down our flesh. Until then, we are called to ardently wage war against sin and temptation and mourn over its presence in our lives. While we live in a world that offers countless reasons to mourn—sickness, loneliness, disease, disappointment, death, and the like— Jesus' blood reminds us to look beyond the consequences of living in a fallen world to our daily struggle with sin. The blood of Christ reminds us never to try to excuse or hide our sin, but rather to cry out, "Wretched man that I am!" (Rom. 7:24).

Believers are called to faithfully fight against our impulse to sin. How? Determine daily to saturate your mind in God's Word and commit yourself to obey it. Faithfully confess your sin in prayer, seeking the grace of repentance to turn from your sin and walk on the path of holiness. Don't give one moment's consideration to temptation, and ardently pray it would depart from you. In your fight against sin, find others that will hold you accountable in thought, word, and deed. For all those who may find themselves in the valley of despair because of their constant fight with sin, comfort is promised (Matt. 5:4). Jesus reminds us, again and again, that sin is no longer our master since we have been washed in the fountain of his precious blood.

Fifth, the blood of Christ reminds us of the necessity of humility. There's a danger in discussing the benefits of the atonement of Christ. There's a possibility that after hearing such abundant blessings that are now ours in Christ, we become prideful.

The Bible is clear that God hates pride because it stands in the way of us enjoying and delighting in him (Prov. 8:13; Ps. 10:4). Self-righteousness can easily creep into a heart that has enjoyed the benefits of redemption and plant seeds of a "haughty spirit" (Prov. 16:18–19). Humility, however, is a defining characteristic of one born again. "Put on then," Paul says, "as God's chosen ones, holy and beloved, compassionate hearts, kindness, humility, meekness, and patience" (Col. 3:12). Not only do we come to Christ for salvation with a humble spirit, but our demeanor, actions, service, and words as believers are characterized by humility. In his classic work *Precious Remedies against Satan's Devices*, Thomas Brooks reminds us of the fruits of humility:

Humility will keep the soul free from many darts cast by Satan and from many erroneous snares spread by him. As low trees and shrubs are free from many violent blasts of wind which shake and rend the taller ones, so humble souls are free from those blasts of error which rend and tear proud, lofty souls. Satan and the world have greater difficulty to fasten errors upon humble souls.[3]

Jesus is our model in this. "The Son of Man came not to be served but to serve" (Matt. 20:38). From gathering little children around him to eating with tax collectors and sinners to washing his disciples' feet, Jesus is the example we are called to emulate. This Christlike humility is to be demonstrated in serving our families, churches, and neighbors. When we sense any pride creeping into our hearts, we must return to the cross and behold the blood that was shed for undeserving sinners.

Sixth, the blood of Christ reminds us of the beautifying work of the Holy Spirit. Salvation isn't simply a get-out-of-hell-free card. It's more beautiful than that. The inward transformation of our affections and heart in salvation is about making us more like Jesus—being made holy. New England pastor Jonathan Edwards preached:

3   Thomas Brooks, *Precious Remedies against Satan's Devices* (Philadelphia, PA: Jonathan Pounder, 1810), 110.

Holiness is the very beauty and loveliness of Jehovah himself. 'Tis the excellency of his excellencies, the beauty of his beauties, the perfection of his infinite perfections, and the glory of his attributes. What an honor, then, must it be to a creature who is infinitely below God, and less than he, to be beautified and adorned with this beauty, with that beauty which is the highest beauty of God himself, even holiness.[4]

The Holy Spirit brings about this beautifying work. Edwards is amazed that God would "sanctify sinners— loathsome and abominable creatures—and make them like to himself."[5]

The holiness for which we are saved is accomplished only through an intense, heartfelt stare at Jesus. We all know what it's like to receive a glaring stare from a parent when we've disobeyed. Words aren't necessary for a reprimand; the stare alone communicates the required level of conformity.

---

4   Jonathan Edwards, *Sermons and Discourses, 1720–1723*, ed. Wilson H. Kimnach, in *The Works of Jonathan Edwards*, vol. 10 (New Haven, CT: Yale University Press, 1992), 430.
5   Edwards, *Sermons and Discourses, 1720–1723*, 430.

Edwards says we need such a sight of the divine beauty of Christ that our hearts and will bow before his loveliness. Naturally, as long as our redeemed souls are encased in sinful flesh, we oppose the Spirit's work of beautifying holiness. But "one glimpse of the moral and spiritual glory of God, and supreme amiableness of Jesus Christ, shining into the heart, overcomes and abolishes this opposition, and inclines the soul to Christ."[6]

When the Spirit causes the beauty of Christ to dawn in our hearts, all opposition to holiness flees, our eyes firmly rivet to his flawless loveliness, and we are made beautiful. A chief work of the Spirit is to bring beauty out of chaos. In creation, the Spirit brought harmony out of formlessness and void (Gen. 1:2). In redemption, the Spirit brings life out of death and sin (John 3:5–6, 8). In sanctification, the Spirit brings beauty out of fallen flesh and wayward hearts (Rom. 8:9–11). Believers become instruments of Christ's beaming radiance in the world through the individual

6   Jonathan Edwards, *Sermons and Discourses, 1743–1758*, ed. Wilson H. Kimnach, in *The Works of Jonathan Edwards*, vol. 25 (New Haven, CT: Yale University Press, 2006), 635.

expressions of the beautifying work of the Holy Spirit.[7]

"No condemnation now I dread"

Understanding the significance of the blood of Christ isn't about "claiming" victory over finances, sickness, and the like. This approach is anti-gospel. Instead, we recognize that through the blood of Christ, we have been given victory through Christ. Through the blood of Christ, we no longer stand condemned in our sin. Through the blood of Christ, we are empowered to walk by the Spirit, mourning over our sin, taking our requests before God in prayer, and living lives of selfless humility. Through the blood of Christ, we victoriously sing with Charles Wesley:

No condemnation now I dread;
Jesus, and all in Him, is mine!
Alive in Him, my living Head,
And clothed in righteousness Divine,
Bold I approach the eternal throne,
And claim the crown, through Christ my own.

7   See Dustin Benge, *The Loveliest Place: The Beauty and Glory of the Church* (Wheaton, IL: Crossway Books, 2022), 65–66.

Bold I approach the eternal throne,
And claim the crown, through Christ my own.[8]

SCRIPTURE

1 Corinthians 10:12–13; Ephesians 4:14–21;
Colossians 3:1–17; 1 John 1:5–10

REFLECTION

1. What does it mean for believers to have victory through the blood of Christ?
2. Why is it vital that believers daily fight sin and temptation?
3. List some practical ways you can cultivate humility in your life.
4. What is the role of the Holy Spirit in our Christian walk?

---

8   Charles Wesley, "And Can It Be That I Should Gain?" (1738).

EPILOGUE

The Gospel

For I am not ashamed of the gospel, for it is the
power of God for salvation to everyone who
believes, to the Jew first and also to the Greek.
For in it the righteousness of God is revealed
from faith for faith, as it is written, "The
righteous shall live by faith."

ROMANS 1:16–17

THIS BOOK IS ABOUT THE GOSPEL—its application and benefits. I want to leave you with the clear message of the gospel as given to us in Scripture.

Throughout the New Testament, the "gospel of God" (Rom. 1:1) is described in many ways:

- "the good news of the kingdom of God" (Luke 16:16)
- "good news ... of Jesus Christ" (Acts 8:12)
- "the gospel of the grace of God" (Acts 20:24)
- "the gospel of his Son" (Rom. 1:9)
- "the gospel of your salvation" (Eph. 1:13)
- "the gospel of the glory of the blessed God" (1 Tim. 1:11).

The word translated "gospel" is the Greek word *euangelion*. The prefix *eu* means "good," and *angelion* means "message." When those two words are merged, *gospel* means "good news." In our fallen and sinful world, we're surrounded by *bad* news at every turn—calamity, disease, hunger, poverty, war, and the list could go on and on. Lest we despair, Scripture cries forth the good news of the gospel.

The gospel isn't an earthly or human-devised message or the product of man's imagination in response to our tragedies. The gospel is a divine and heavenly message. Paul begins his letter to the church in Rome by defining the gospel as the "gospel *of God*" (Rom. 1:1).

Chapter after chapter of this book points to God as the

initiator and giver of the gospel. The gospel is about *God's* holiness, wrath, justice, love, grace, mercy, and righteousness.

Defining the Gospel

We're faced with countless artificial definitions of the gospel; these are of no interest to us. We need to know how God defines the gospel in Scripture. What does it mean for him to say, "For God so loved the world, that he gave his only Son, that whoever believes in him should not perish but have eternal life" (John 3:16)?

The gospel is the good news of salvation through God's Son, Jesus Christ. It is the message that God rescues sinners from his wrath against sin through the sacrificial, substitutionary death of Jesus Christ upon the cross and his triumphant resurrection from the dead. This is the good news.

We will never hear anything more surpassingly glorious than the truth that Jesus Christ is a willing Savior of sinners.

What precisely is the "good news" of the gospel?

God sent his Son, the second person of the Trinity, the Lord Jesus Christ, to rescue sinners. He was born of a virgin and lived a sinless, perfect, obedient life under the law. He was crucified on a cross as a substitute to pay the penalty of God's wrath against the sins of all those who would ever believe. In his body, he bore the punishment due to sinners on that cross, and his perfect righteousness was imputed to them, making them acceptable in the sight of God. He was buried in a borrowed tomb and, on the third day, rose from the dead. He ascended back to heaven, the realm of divine authority and power, to sit at the of his Father's right hand and there to intercede for all believers. Now, everyone who by faith "calls on the name of the Lord will be saved" (Rom. 10:13).

Now, let's unpack this statement by offering concise statements with accompanying Bible verses.

We Have Rejected God in Sin

Every human being has been created in the image of God, but because of the fall of Adam and Eve, we are separated from God because of sin.

God created man in his own image, in the image of God he created him; male and female he created them. (Gen. 1:27)

When the woman saw that the tree was good for food,

and that it was a delight to the eyes, and that the tree was to be desired to make one wise, she took of its fruit and ate, and she also gave some to her husband who was with her, and he ate. Then the eyes of both were opened, and they knew that they were naked. And they sewed fig leaves together and made themselves loincloths. (Gen. 3:6–7)

For all have sinned and fall short of the glory of God. (Rom. 3:23)

God's perfect holiness and justice demand that sin be punished by eternal death. As a sinner, because we do not have a right standing with God and are incapable of performing any good works that please him, apart from Jesus Christ, we will suffer God's wrath.

For the wrath of God is revealed from heaven against all ungodliness and unrighteousness of men, who by their unrighteousness suppress the truth. (Rom. 1:18)

For the wages of sin is death, but the free gift of God is

eternal life in Christ Jesus our Lord. (Rom 6:23).

We have all become like one who is unclean, and all our righteous deeds are like a polluted garment. We all fade like a leaf, and our iniquities, like the wind, take us away. (Isa. 64:6)

God Has Made Provision through Christ

God sent Jesus Christ to do what we cannot do for ourselves. Jesus lived a sinless life, took upon himself God's penalty for sin, died a substitutionary death on the cross, conquered death by rising again, and ascended to God's right hand in power and authority.

Christ redeemed us from the curse of the law by becoming a curse for us—for it is written, "Cursed is everyone who is hanged on a tree." (Gal. 3:13)

[Christ] himself bore our sins in his body on the tree, that we might die to sin and live to righteousness. By his wounds you have been healed. (1 Pet. 2:24)

The Son of Man must be delivered into the hands of sinful men and be crucified and on the third day rise. (Luke 24:7)

When Christ had offered for all time a single sacrifice for sins, he sat down at the right hand of God. (Heb. 10:12)

We Must Receive Christ by Faith

We must be born again to be forgiven of sin and come into right standing before God. We must repent of our sin and, by faith, believe in the Lord Jesus Christ by trusting him as the only way of salvation.

Truly, truly, I say to you, unless one is born again he cannot see the kingdom of God. (John 3:3)

Jesus said to him, "I am the way, and the truth, and the life. No one comes to the Father except through me." (John 14:6)

Repent therefore, and turn back, that your sins may be blotted out. (Acts 3:19)

If you confess with your mouth that Jesus is Lord

and believe in your heart that God raised him from the dead, you will be saved. For with the heart one believes and is justified, and with the mouth one confesses and is saved. (Rom. 10:9–10)

God Has Promised to Save

God promises that when we repent of our sin and by faith believe in Jesus Christ, we're saved, forgiven for all our sins, and welcomed into the family of God.

> Since we have been justified by faith, we have peace with God through our Lord Jesus Christ. (Rom. 5:1)

> [The Father] has delivered us from the domain of darkness and transferred us to the kingdom of his beloved Son, in whom we have redemption, the forgiveness of sins. (Col. 1:13–14)

> My sheep hear my voice, and I know them, and they follow me. I give them eternal life, and they will never perish, and no one will snatch them out of my hand. My Father, who has given them to me, is greater than

all, and no one is able to snatch them out of the Father's hand. (John 10:27–29)

See what kind of love the Father has given to us, that we should be called children of God; and so we are. (1 John 3:1)

We Must Live for Christ

Beginning a new life in Jesus Christ, our Lord, means that we start living for him and in obedience to him. Following Christ includes making a public profession of our faith, joining fellowship with other believers in a local church, and seeking to grow more like Christ by reading the Bible, praying, and living all of life for him.

For just as the body is one and has many members, and all the members of the body, though many, are one body, so it is with Christ. (1 Cor. 12:12)

Let us consider how to stir up one another to love and good works, not neglecting to meet together, as is the habit of some, but encouraging one another, and all the more as you see the Day drawing near. (Heb. 10:24–25)

Therefore, if anyone is in Christ, he is a new creation. The old has passed away; behold, the new has come. (2 Cor. 5:17)

By this we know that we have come to know him, if we keep his commandments. (1 John 2:3)

Grow in the grace and knowledge of our Lord and Savior Jesus Christ. (2 Pet. 3:18)

This is the gospel.

While this book has explained the *benefits* of the atonement of Christ, the benefits themselves are not the gospel. The gospel is a message about historical events that took place in space and time. The gospel is a person—Jesus Christ—and the story of what he came to do in place of sinners. Peter once stood before the ruling Jewish council and boldly declared, "There is no other name under heaven given among men by which we must be saved" (Acts 4:12). Likewise, Paul maintained that "there is one God, and there is one mediator between God and men, the man Christ Jesus" (1 Tim. 2:5). The gospel of Jesus Christ is the only gospel that will reconcile us to God and bring us peace and salvation.

If you have further questions about the gospel or have repented of your sins and placed faith in Christ, I urge you to find a local church that preaches the truth of Scripture and talk to a pastor about what has happened in your life.

If you are already a believer, rejoice in the gospel once again and the benefits that are ours through Christ. Meditate upon God's provision for you in Christ by thanking him, living a faithful and obedient life, and sharing the gospel with others. The German Reformer Martin Luther wrote,

So the *evangel* (gospel) of God ... is also a good message and report. The gospel has resounded in all the world, proclaimed by the apostles. It tells of a true David who fought with sin, death, and the devil, overcame them, and thereby delivered, without any merit of their own, all those who were held captive in sin, were plagued by death, and were overpowered by the devil. He made them righteous, gave them life, and saved them.[1]

The blood of Christ changes everything.

---

1   Ewald Plass, *What Luther Says: A Practical In-Home Anthology for the Active Christian* (St. Louis: Concordia, 1959), 561.

ACKNOWLEDGEMENTS

This book would not have been possible without the following people:

Chance Faulkner, who originally encouraged me to write this book, after seeing one of my Twitter posts listing the benefits of the atonement of Christ.

Rebecca Rine, whom I have had the privilege of working with for many years, whose keen editorial eye and skillful suggestions always elevate my writing to be more precise and clearer.

Michael A.G. Haykin, Nate Pickowicz, Chance Faulkner, Michael Staton, Justin Williams, and Grant Castleberry all read my initial manuscript and made beneficial comments and recommendations that shaped the final work.

My dear wife, Molli, whose constant encouragement, and prayers always uphold me through the writing process, ministry, and life.

SCRIPTURE INDEX

MORE TITLES
AVAILABLE AT:

HESEDANDEMET.COM

CPSIA information can be obtained
at www.ICGtesting.com
Printed in the USA
JSHW081948101122
32872JS00004B/22